Reiki in the Saddle

By Sarah Berrisford

Published by Pinchbeck Press

www.pinchbeckpress.com
email: taggart@reiki-evolution.co.uk

ISBN 978-0-9563168-7-5

Introduction

This book is related to my findings of using Reiki whilst horse riding, plus exercises we can use from the ground.

I have compiled experiences and instructions, which I have used myself and also which have been used by my students. The instructions detailed in each section do not need to be followed by the letter, they are simply a guide, so if something I have written doesn't quite resonate for you, please try it in a slightly different way.

Some of the exercises in this book are used within my Equine Reiki courses, just contained in a slightly different context, students have come along to the courses and told me 'I can't do that!' This was just the initial reaction of reading what they were going to do. When they actually put it into practice, they realised just how simple, easy, yet effective it can be. So don't be put off – just give it a go!

Although the exercises in this book are aimed at persons who have already completed the Reiki 1st Degree, I hope that those who read this book and haven't any Reiki experience can see the positive aspects of learning Reiki.

I hope this book brings you further joy and happiness within your riding.

If we can do it together,
With feeling and heart,
We can achieve with each other,
What we can't apart.

Reiki: What is it?

When we talk about Reiki, most people have some concept that we are working with energy to aid the recipients own healing capacity. This is true of course, however, there is much more to Reiki than healing.

Those who practice Reiki try to live by Mikao Usui's precepts:

Just for today
Do not anger
Do not worry
Be humble
Be honest in your dealings with people
Be compassionate towards yourself and others

The precepts are described as 'The secret method of inviting happiness through many blessings'.

In my work with horses I interpret the precepts in the following ways:

Just for today, do not anger: many people have said to me that this doesn't apply to their relationship with their horse; they don't feel angry with their horse. However, if you take a closer look into the deeper meaning, 'do not anger' in the equestrian world, could be translated into, do not become frustrated with yourself or your horse. When things are not quite going to plan, we can become quite frustrated with ourselves, so this part of the precepts, can be just as much about you as it is the horse.

Just for today, do not worry: it is all too easy to worry about our horses. We worry that we are not doing things correctly, or that we are not as good as others. For me, this section of the precepts, relates to belief in oneself around horses. We need to believe in ourselves, not worry about other people, or whether we are doing things the same way as other people that seem to have reached that goal you have been striving for - if we do not believe in ourselves then how can we expect our horses too.

Just for today, be humble: Well this is an easy one! When the ego comes into play, horses love to show you up! If you get too big for your boots, they can bring you down in the drop of a hat. Just to clarify this point, I am not saying that you shouldn't be proud of yourself for achievements or enjoy how the horse works with you, but rather if a person becomes obsessed with how wonderful they are, so much better than other people, the horse will lose respect for them.

Just for today, be honest in your dealings with people: this part of the precepts is about honesty with yourself, your horse and others. My main focus is the honesty between horse and rider. When we are honest with the horse, he will try to help us, for example, if we are feeling nervous and say to the horse 'I am feeling nervous' please look after me', the horse will usually look after you, rather than if you hide emotions from the horse, he will not trust you, horses are very open animals, they do not understand the concept of hiding feelings and emotions, so a person hiding what they are feeling can easily be seen as a threat or weak, rather than a person that is open is seen as 'being'.

Just for today, be compassionate towards yourself and others: This one speaks for itself, show your horse and yourself compassion. Most horse owners have a good understanding of how their horse is feeling, but we also need to look deep inside ourselves on a regular basis and check how we are really feeling, with the desire to relieve any suffering we are going through, emotionally or physically, it is important for the horse to know that his owner is emotionally well, and if you are not, remember – be honest in your dealing with your horse!

Learning Reiki

I think that learning Reiki is personal experience in that we are drawn to a particular person or way of using the energy that will suit us. There are many Reiki teachers all over the country, who can be found through a simple search on 'google'. Of course, I recommend Reiki Evolution and love their simple and undogmatic approach.

How can energy work improve your riding?

Through working with energy whilst riding and also in general around our horses we are not only aiming to improve the horses way of going, but also improving our overall relationship with the horse, gaining an in depth knowledge of how we can easily portray to the horse what we would like of him.

Using energy, visualisation and intent can help improve every aspect of riding; whatever the problem, we can find a solution through use of energy. It is important to remember that in any situation, the more we worry about it, or think about what is going wrong, the more energy we are giving to the unwanted situation. Instead we need to think positively, with a joyful outlook, imagining what we want – not what we don't want.

When we visualise or think about what we want, we need to take the neediness away; so we are not thinking we really 'need' this to happen, instead we are thinking about what we would like and feeling happiness. An easy way to achieve this is simply by smiling whilst we are thinking.

What can I do if I find visualisation hard?

Firstly, you can simply think of the situation instead. You could think of yourself talking excitedly about the situation to a friend, what type of things would you say? You could also think of others talking about improvements; happy for you that you have achieved them.

Visualisation is important. It is something anyone can do; just sometimes it can take a bit of practice.

An exercise to help with visualisation:

- Sit comfortably on a chair
- Take some deep breaths to help you relax
- Focus on an object in front of you (try to pick something colourful or that has meaning to you – a pretty picture perhaps)
- Take in everything about the picture, look at the lines, the colours, the feeling you get from the picture
- Close your eyes and look up for a couple of seconds
- Now try to imagine the outline of that picture, think of the feeling the picture gave you and try to bring back that feeling whilst imagining the outline.

- Once you have an outline or silhouette of the picture, open your eyes again. Take in the colour of the picture.
- Close your eyes again, look up for a couple of seconds, activating the third eye.
- See the outline of the picture again and now try to colour the picture in, start with the main colour of the picture and gradually progress.

By practising the above exercise, even if only the outline of the picture or the silhouette of the object, you will gradually progress in your visualization skills.

Energy; what is it? And how can I use it?

Energy is everywhere, we all use energy and we all have the ability to sense energy, however, this important and very natural skill, has been somewhat conditioned out of us, pushed somewhere deep within as it seems unneeded in this day and age – how wrong is that statement?!

Energy is really quite simple to understand; have you ever had an unexplained feeling about a person or a situation, which has turned out you had good reason for? This is sensing the energy.

Most horse persons are more aware of energy; they need to be in order to work with the horse. We know that a horse may be standing still, yet we can sense whether this is due to calmness, nervousness or brimming with excitement.

When using Reiki we use this same energy that we sense in others, we practice energy cultivating techniques to improve our body as a channel this in turn allows us to use the energy around us simply, yet effectively.

Everything is made up of energy; we are simply focusing this energy towards a positive result.

Improving the Rider-Horse relationship

To improve the relationship between horse and rider, we need to improve the connection they have with each other, helping both to understand their partner.

The first and perhaps most obvious way to approach this, is to use HSZSN. Pronounced: 'Hon Shay Zay Show Nen' this symbol represents Oneness.

The Hon Sha Ze Sho Nen symbol is the given way of experiencing the state of oneness. We are all one. This symbol is also seen as the distant healing symbol, being used as a way to 'connect' to others.

The HSZSN symbol does not produce an energy, rather it elicits a state within the practitioner; a state of oneness where you can move beyond time and space.

Drawing Instructions HSZSN

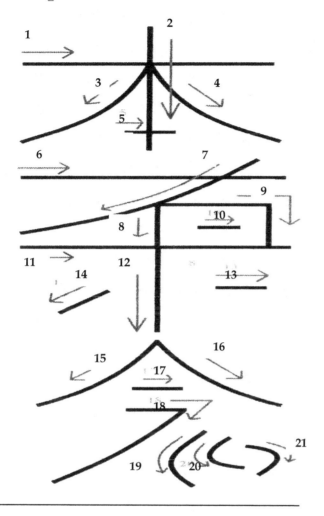

There are a few ways we could use the symbol,

- We could visualize it above ourselves or the person riding the horse
- We could use it in the stable or whilst around the horse on the ground

- We could use it distantly

In fact you could use this symbol in anyway that pops into your head, if you are reading this and thinking "I'd like to use it like…." Then that's the way for you to use it, that's your intuition telling you the best way of what will work for you. This doesn't mean that this will be the exact same way every time you come to use the symbol.

Also, it is important to remember that you don't need to use the symbol whilst in the process of doing something, for example, if you would like to improve the connection between horse and rider, you can carry out the exercise from the ground, distantly or whilst the rider is on board, just by using your intent.

Using HSZSN for a horse and rider

1) Connect to Reiki in the way you are accustomed to.
2) Bring energy down through your crown to your Tanden, feeling the energy build in your Tanden and then spread throughout your body, and then out of your body in all directions.
3) Visualize the HSZSN symbol above the rider and horse, say the name 3 times to empower it.

4) Allow the energy of the HSZSN symbol to surround the horse and rider

5) Just let this visualisation carry on for as long as you feel necessary. It may be 5 minutes or it may be 20 minutes, let your intuition guide you as to how long you should keep it up.

6) When you have finished, allow the HSZSN symbol to stay with the horse and rider, with the intent that it will stay with them and carry on working, even when you leave.

Using HSZSN for yourself whilst riding

1) Before you mount your horse, connect to Reiki in the way you are accustomed to. For some practitioners, you will be able to connect to Reiki whilst on the horse, but for others who perhaps have certain rituals before commencing, it may be a lot easier to do this before you mount up.

2) Once mounted you can either imagine the HSZSN symbol in the air above you and the horse or you could draw it in front of you with your hand or fingers and say the name 3 times to empower it.

3) Do this at the beginning of the session, with the intent that the symbol will stay there throughout your ride.

4) Every so often during your ride, just let your attention drift to the symbol which is connecting you and your horse even more deeply, every time you think of it.

Using HSZSN on the ground

1) Ask the owner to stand a few feet away from the horse, this can be in the stable or outside
2) Connect to Reiki
3) Bring the energy down in to your Tanden
4) Now draw the HSZSN symbol in between the horse and owner, draw it large and slowly, with your palm, being careful not to shock the horse as you draw!
5) Set your intent as to what area you would like to see more connection and a better understanding if you have one.
6) Say the name 3 times to empower it and allow the energy to make a bubble around the horse ad owner, connecting them together as one.

You can also do this exercise for yourself. You simply stand in place of the owner and carry out the exercise

Using HSZSN distantly

1) Connect to Reiki
2) Think of the horse and owner
3) Visualize the HSZSN over or near the horse and rider
4) Say the name 3 times to empower it
5) Allow any Reiki to flow through; healing any issues, whilst at the same time the HSZSN symbol is working its magic to help the connection and relationship.

These are all very simple exercises, which you can alter to make your own if you wish and resonate well with your way of working.

Example

Whilst riding my horse Thunder, I felt that his brain was else where. He didn't pay attention to me and to be honest, I felt that I was nagging him to do something that he had little interest in. I wasn't enjoying riding as I felt that I was doing something wrong. I decided to try using the HSZSN symbol; I stood next to Thunder and imagined the HSZSN symbol above us, with the oneness energy surrounding us.

I got on Thunder and started to walk around the arena, I took some deep breaths and just affirmed to myself that the HSZSN symbol would be with us throughout the ride.

Thunder seemed to pick up in his attitude; he began to walk faster and asked if he could go into trot, he suddenly began to enjoy his work, after our session in the arena, I took Thunder for a short hack as I had the feeling that he also wanted to get out and about, we had a lovely hack.

I felt that using the HSZSN symbol for horse and rider helped me more than then horse on this occasion, connecting to the symbol made me realise that it wasn't just Thunder who seemed switched off, it was me who was 'not present' during our riding, it was me who was thinking about other things instead of enjoying my time with Thunder.

I now use the HSZSN symbol for a couple of minutes before I ride, it really helps me to switch off from other things that are going on in my life and just enjoy my time with my horse.
Kylie Rand

Another way to aid the relationship between rider and horse is to open their chakras to each other. Please note you can also use these exercises to help animals get along better with each other, this applies to all types of animals; horse to horse, human to human, horse to dog and the list goes on…

The Chakras

Location of Chakras

The diagram below gives you an idea of where the chakras are located on the horse.

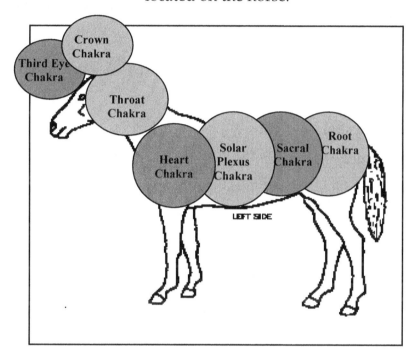

What is a Chakra?

Chakra is a Sanskrit word meaning wheel; it refers to the seven energy centers in our body. The chakras regulate the flow of energy through our energy system.

Each sense, feeling and experience is divided into seven categories and therefore allocated to a specific chakra. When a person's chakras are dull or aren't spinning properly, the emotional, physical and mental body will not be working in harmony with each other.

Balanced chakras results in optimal health and vitality.

Each of the seven main chakras is comprised of seven levels, they are:

1) Physical

2) Emotional

3) Mental

4) Causal (cause and effect)

5) Intuitive and/ or psychic

6) Spiritual

7) Transcendental or beyond that of the physical realm

The Base/ Root Chakra

Security, trust, the home and work are all connected with the root chakra; the root is where life begins. This chakra also reflects a beings connection to Mother Earth

Colour – Red

Stones associated – Garnet, Ruby, Smoky Quartz

Location – Located at the base of the animal spine (near the tail)

Influences – Adrenal glands, spine, bones (marrow), legs, back feet, kidneys, colon, anus and tail.

Sense - Sense of smell is covered by this chakra

Effects of Reiki – Channeling Reiki to the Root Chakra helps to balance the physical animal body and clear out fears, insecurity and anger. Also helps to relieve spinal tension, constipation, anemia's, urinary incontinence and any related problems associated with the areas mentioned under influences.

The Sacral Chakra

This chakra is linked to emotions and your willingness to feel your emotions.

Colour - Orange

Stones associated – Moonstone, Topaz, Opal

Location – Located in the lower abdominal area

Influences – Genital, pelvis, reproductive organs, large and small intestines, stomach, sacrum and lumbar vertebrae.

Sense – The sense of taste and appetite are associated with this chakra

Effects of Reiki – Reiki helps to relieve sexual difficulties, impotence, release tension, increase male potency, heal problems with uterus or bladder and any related problems associated with the areas mentioned under influences.

The Solar Plexus Chakra

Power, control and mental activity are associated with this chakra. It is linked to personality. The power centre is connected to the solar plexus. This is the chakra from which the animals power and mastery of self originates.

Colour - Yellow

Stones associated – Tigers Eye, Amber, Citrine

Location – Located in the middle abdominal region

Influences – Stomach, gallbladder, pancreas, liver, diaphragm, kidneys, nervous system and lumbar vertebrae

Sense - Eyesight

Effects of Reiki – Reiki helps to clear digestive disorders, increase appetite, increase energy, eliminate fatigue and any related problems associated with the areas mentioned under influences.

The Heart Chakra

The heart chakra is associated with the heart and is the chakra of love and compassion.

Colour - green

Stones associated – Emerald, Green Jade, Rose Quartz

Location – Located in the centre of the chest

Influences – Heart, blood circulation, lower lungs, chest, thoracic vertebrae, immune system

Sense – Touch and the sensitivity that comes from being touched

Effects of Reiki – Reiki helps to alleviate heart and circulatory problems, immune system dysfunctions, emotional instability, anger. Energizes the blood and circulation. Instills harmony, balance, contentment, peace and happiness. Helps with other problems associated with areas mentioned under influences.

The Throat Chakra

The throat chakra is related to communication and creativity.

Colour - Blue

Stones associated – Blue Topaz, Turquoise, Aquamarine

Location – Located in the throat

Influences – Thyroid, lungs, respiratory system, forelegs, feet, throat, mouth, vocal chords

Sense - Hearing

Effects of Reiki – Reiki helps to alleviate depression, thyroid problems, vocal problems, hair loss, abnormal weight gain or loss, problems with metabolism, and any related problems associated with the areas mentioned under influences.

The Third Eye Chakra

This is the chakra of animal thinking and emotions

Colour - Indigo

Stones associated– Blue Sapphire, Clear Quartz, Tourmaline

Location – Located between the eyes.

Sense – It is related to seeing, both physically and intuitively and tunes in to our psychic ability.

Effects of Reiki – Reiki helps to alleviate headaches, problems with the eyes, tension, hyperactivity, jumpiness and any related problems associated with thinking and emotions.

The Crown Chakra

This chakra controls every aspect of the animal body and mind. It is also known as the cosmic consciousness centre. It is associated with the brain and nervous system.

Colour – Violet/ purple

Stones associated – Amethyst, Clear Quartz, Opal.

Location – Located on top of the head.

Effects of Reiki – Reiki helps to alleviate confusion, senility depression, malaise and convulsions. This chakra gives a sense of empathy and unity and is calming when centered on.

During the day of the course, you will have the chance to practice experiencing a horse's chakras. You can practice on friends and family before attending the course if you wish.

How to see the chakras

1)   Sit or stand comfortably. Close your eyes.

2)   Take a few long deep breathes and centre yourself.

3)   Feel the energy entering through your crown, coming down the middle of your body and filling your Tanden.

4)   Feel the energy building in your Tanden. We work from the Tanden.

5)   Look through your third eye and allow yourself to see each chakra.

6)   If the horse comes over to you and presents himself forward whilst you are channeling Reiki to one of his chakras, carry on sending Reiki to that particular chakra. The horse is saying; ok you've hit the spot, now I'd like it a bit closer!

People experience chakras in different ways, some see them all straight away, with breath taking colours, others see objects or symbols in the chakra and some find that they can see the chakra by imagining they open a lid or unfold petals etc and look inside to see each chakra individually.

Some chakras may appear sluggish or dull, we can send Reiki into the chakra to speed it up or make it more vibrant and the same is also possible for the opposite; if a chakra is spinning too fast or irregularly. With your hands in the prayer position or relaxed down by your sides channel Reiki towards the horse and to his chakras.

You do not need to be standing with your hands hovering over the horse; we can treat the horse's chakras using our intent, either next to the horse, away from the horse in the stable or even over the stable door. In fact we can even treat the horse's chakras using Distant Healing.

You do not need to be able to 'see' chakras to be able to work with them. All you need to do is to use your intent, so we say "I'm sending Reiki to the Root Chakra to bring it to its optimum functioning" and this is enough to treat the Root Chakra.

During the next exercise we will be opening the chakras and joining the energies together, when animals are harmonious, they naturally share energy with each other, so in effect we are giving this process a 'helping hand'.

It is best to carry out this exercise when the horse has time to relax, so preferably not whilst being ridden or just before work, as he may be a little too laid back straight after his Reiki treatment

Again, it is possible to do this distantly, in person or with the horse whilst the owner is separate.

Connecting the Horse and Riders Chakras

1) Connect to Reiki in your preferred way

2) Close your eyes and focus on the horses Root Chakra, think of the root chakra being bright and shining out

3) Now focus on the persons Root Chakra (if the person is not present just imagine that they are) see the Root Chakra shining out brightly

4) Next focus your intent on the horse's Sacral Chakra, and then the persons Sacral Chakra, let them shine brightly, bringing them to their optimum functioning. (Please note you don't need to keep thinking of the Chakra we've worked on previously, just focus on 1 chakra at a time)

5) Next go to the horse's Solar Plexus, and persons Solar Plexus, seeing them shine brightly

6) Next on to the Heart Chakra, first the horse's and then the persons, seeing this chakra becoming stronger with love on each beat

7) Next on to the horse's Throat Chakra, and then the owners

8) Next focus on the Third Eye Chakra, allowing this to shine brightly on the horse and person

9) Finally the Crown Chakra; let your intent bring the chakra to its optimum functioning on horse and owner.

10) Now it is time to imagine both horse and owner standing next to each other, focus on each chakra in turn, starting with the Root Chakra, the chakras are already nice and bold, shining light and energy brightly, reaching out, the horse and persons Root Chakras are shining out towards each other, as these lights touch the energy between both is joined, with understanding and love.

11) Take your time working through the Chakras, repeating the step above allowing each Chakra to touch and become one

Example

I have used the chakra merging exercise a few times. On the first occasion, I tried this meditation with two of my horses whom were not getting on very well. Although there wasn't any true nastiness, they would constantly pull faces and seemed intolerant of each other.

On the first day of merging the chakras, I did not notice very much happening, all seemed quite normal, I went to bed that night feeling a little disappointed as I had liked the sound of this exercise and had thought it was going to work.

As I lay in bed I imagined the chakras merging again and then promptly fell asleep!

When I went out to feed the horses in the morning, the two horses were standing next to each other dozing – this was not the norm for these two. By the end of the week, the horses had made friends, they weren't best friends, but they had a certain liking for each other that had previously been unapparent.

After the above success, I wanted to try this exercise again, this time I used it on one of my clients and her horse. They seemed to be going in opposite directions, what ever one wanted to do, the other would object!

There was a difference straight away, it was really amazing to see how they suddenly seemed to connect, the rider began to understand her horse and in turn the horse began to respect the rider. After 3 sessions of merging the chakras, the horse and rider looked like a completely different pair, it was wonderful!
Kelly Smith

Exercise to improve the connection with your horse

Below, one of my students Elinor has kindly shared an exercise she uses to improve the connection between horse and human, which also involves working with the chakras.

We all desire a closer connection with our horses and can get disappointed and frustrated when they don't seem to be on 'our' wavelength. (It's more likely that we are not on 'their' wavelength!) Thinking back – I could not remember when I last spent 'quality time' with my horse. (I mean time when I was not demanding anything from her at all. No riding, working from the ground, grooming etc.) Time always seemed in short supply when trying to juggle all my home and work responsibilities. So I resolved to have some 'down time' we could share together, with no pressure and no expectations. Just be in the 'now' – in the moment – just me with my horse.

My mare, Sophie, was loose in the Indoor school as we had been doing some clicker training. She loves clicker-work (food rewards – great!) and her 'toys' - but as it is best not to train for longer than 10 minutes in one session, there were 50 minutes left of the hour I'd booked. Sitting on the mounting block, I watched Sophie wandering round looking for dropped treats. After a while I had the idea to do a Reiki meditation – and take her with me!

* * * * *

When I had finished I opened my eyes and she was in the middle of the arena, head lowered. As I looked at her she walked towards me and nuzzled me. (This is unusual – she is not a 'cuddly' mare and can be quite aloof.) Had she really shared my meditation? Had she been aware of the Reiki energy? Who knows – but it was very pleasant and I have since tried to replicate and adapt it and I certainly feel closer to her. Sometimes I do this whilst sending hands-on Reiki, but usually I just find somewhere safe to sit in her company. The last time I did this meditation, Sophie seemed to let me know when she was 'balanced' in each chakra by 'licking and chewing', and at the end gave a huge sigh (and left a huge pile of droppings!) Of course it is possible to do this from the comfort of your own home by the Distant Reiki method – but it is much more rewarding to be physically together so you can be aware of the horse's reactions. Ideally it is nice to spend about 30 or so minutes on this, but I have 'cantered through it' when pushed for time and it still feels beneficial.

Shared Reiki Meditation/ Chakra Balance

Find a place where you and your horse are safe and unlikely to be interrupted. (It still works even with all the noises associated with a busy yard – you get used to being able to 'zone out' and focus on your thoughts.) This can be with the horse loose in the stable or out in the field. If it is safe to do so, close your eyes.

Start up Reiki in your usual way and ask the horse's permission to send Reiki. Intend that the energy will be for the horse's highest good, and the highest good of your relationship.

Connect using HSZSN. Imagine a bridge of light connecting your heart to that of the horse. Now focus on your breathing. Breathe in for 4 counts, hold for 4 counts, and exhale gently over 8 counts - do this sequence at least three times. Imagine that with each inhalation Reiki energy and light enter your crown, flow down your body and into the Tanden. Allow your body to relax with every 'out' breath, intending that the energy and light expand to surround you and your horse.

In your imagination, create a perfect place where you can be with your horse, perhaps a large grassy area … other horses nearby, quietly grazing … you are aware of birdsong and the humming of insects (though they will not bother you or the horses!) … warm sunshine and a gentle breeze to keep you both comfortable. This is a safe place. You have all the time you need. It is peaceful and you feel calm and happy here. Put in the details ... what colour is your horse? What are you wearing? Can you smell the sweet grass? Are there any trees around? (Use all your senses to make this as vivid and detailed as possible.)

When you are ready, envisage a huge rainbow in the field just ahead of you. The seven colours are transparent, each gradually merging with the colour next to it. It is beautiful and makes you feel good. Normally when you walk towards rainbows they appear to move away elusively – but here the colours stay put, shimmering but strong.

Walk slowly towards the rainbow. Your horse is walking close by your side. Walk together into the red light and stop for a while. Imagine this red light affecting everything you see, it is like looking through glasses with coloured lenses. The horse grazes on the red grass. Intend that the red-coloured energy is absorbed by both your base charkas, bringing each into optimal balance.

When you feel the time is right, step into the orange section of the rainbow. Everything you see has an orange tint. The horse follows you and happily crops the orange-coloured grass as you imagine the orange light entering both your sacral charkas, bringing them into optimal balance. Stay in this colour until your intuition tells you it is time to move forward.

Take a few steps onwards with your horse and experience the yellow light. Look around and notice the way this light changes things - everything glows like sunshine. Whilst your horse samples the yellow grass, intend that this colour enters your solar plexus chakras and brings them into perfect balance. You feel relaxed and at peace.

Your horse walks forwards to the green grass in the next part of the spectrum and you follow step by step until you are both engulfed in green light. It is pleasant and fresh. You may decide to sit down here for a while, though you are not tired. Here the heart chakras of both equine and human are restored to balance. You feel well and content, listening to the steady tearing and munching sounds as your horse eats. All is well. This is a good place to be. No thoughts of past concerns or future worries can reach you. You are both at the heart of the rainbow and you feel connected through this shared experience. You can stay here as long as you like – there is no need to rush.

You notice a blue light ahead and get up to walk into it and your companion follows you. Everything appears a lovely sky-blue. Your throat chakras absorb the blue energy and are revitalised and balanced. The blue grass, full of beneficial herbs, tastes good and your horse eats contentedly.

A few steps further on, the light becomes a deeper indigo blue. Allow this new colour to enter your brow chakra and imagine it entering the horse's brow chakra also. You look at your horse in your mind's eye and smile – grass is grass whatever colour it appears to be, it all tastes wonderful!

Once again you slowly walk forwards, accompanied by your equine friend. Now the light and everything you see is violet. The colour is translucent and sparkles on the grass. The violet grass may look strange, but to the horse it tastes delicious. As you continue to breathe deeply, your crown chakra becomes filled with this violet energy. Intend that the violet light is absorbed by your horse's crown chakra. Optimum balance is restored and you both feel fantastic.

The rainbow shimmers suddenly and all the colours merge and dissolve into a bright white light. The horse's brachial chakra comes into balance. The horse looks at you and comes towards you, head lowered, relaxed.

You now walk out of the white light and back into the sunshine. Spend some time enjoying the calmness and peace – just you and your horse together.

When you are ready thank your horse for being with you and sharing your meditation. Gently erase the bridge of light connecting your hearts and separate the light surrounding you both, so that you each have your own sphere of light. Thank any guides you may have invited along to assist then disconnect from the Reiki energy. (Kenyoku-ho : dry bathing.)
Take some deep breaths and open your eyes. Smile!

Elinor Mary Thomas
www.sofarsogoodtherapy.co.uk

Tacking up

Many horses nowadays have issues with being tacked up, for some it is just a small flinch as you do the girth up, for others it is a full blown problem.

To over come this we can spend some time Reiki-ing these objects, whether this be the saddle, bridle, girth, or any of the parts of these.

We can also Reiki the process of putting each piece of equipment on the horse.

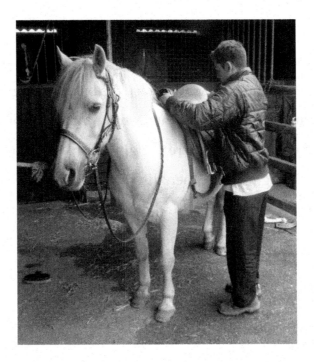

The effects of this exercise usually build up over time, often we start to see results after 3 or 4 sessions. The good thing about these sessions is that they only take 5 minutes or less and they are really simple!

1) Stand by the piece of tack
2) Connect to Reiki

3) Set your intent " I am Reiki-ing the saddle so that the horse likes it being put on his back" We then imagine the saddle being put on the horses back and the horse being fine with it

4) To finish we imagine a golden ball of light surrounding the saddle.

We can also use the same exercise as above, but change the intent, so on step 3, we can say "I am Reiki-ing the saddle, so that when it is placed on the horses back, the energy is there to give the nicest possible ride for the horse and rider".

Example

When Sarah told me I could Reiki my tack, I thought "that's pushing it a bit" how can Reiki work on an object?? My tack isn't a living thing! Sarah told me to give it a go, so I stood in the tack shed, imagining a golden ball of light around my saddle, I did feel a bit silly!

Then the fun began, as I placed the saddle on my horses back, he turned his head to me and nodded, usually he just stands half asleep whilst having his tack put on.

As soon as I mounted, I felt that he was carrying me well, it felt a bit like he was enjoying the feeling of the saddle on his back, however, I was still a bit skeptical...

Once we had warmed up he began to show off to me, if I asked for a little Travers he would give me a perfect one straight away. All of the movements felt very easy for him.

I then realised as I was riding around that my back was feeling more supple and my seat was the lightest it had ever felt, yet some how I was a part of the horse sitting within him. Needless to say, I very much enjoyed my ride!

When I took the saddle off my horse, he turned and touched it with his nose and then looked at me deeply in the eyes – I now Reiki my saddle on a regular basis!
Claire Brown

Hacking

I am often asked about Reiki exercises to help horses and riders whilst out hacking, the following are the most common to occur and ways to help using energy

Experience

How the scenery changes in such a short time!

I took my just 5yr old out and I am lucky enough to go straight out from the yard into the woods, although they aren't very large, it's great for starting the youngsters off.

I thought we would follow the bottom route as it wouldn't be as mushy after all the rain, and also she has always found it more "spooky".. so I thought it would be a great training exercise for her. I usually send her Reiki whilst grooming and tacking her up, which works really well, as she is a "thinker" and with her hereditary stress lines, a good chance of being an internal worrier, although she doesn't show it by losing weight that's for sure!

Well, with all the new greenery that's going bonkers growing, it was SOOO scary and sooo different you would have thought we were on a new planet, talk about "poopy pants"! After a few minutes, just stopped and looking, we proceeded up the very overgrown lane, which has a Boarding Kennels on one side and a hedge, trees and open field on the other, Frazzel heard all the dogs barking and folks shouting and stopped dead in her tracks, eyes popping, head and neck totally rigid, and then bless her, she started shaking.....this she has never done since I have started riding her out, which is now a good 5 months or so, I sat talking to her and decided that Reiki was called for, so after a few deep breaths I connected to the energy and just let it flow down over both of us, putting a big bubble of white light around us........we stayed on the spot for about 3/4mins, after which she stopped shaking and started to lower her head, I had also held my hand against her neck for her to take the energy and not feel that she was on her own.

We travelled further up the lane, still looking at everything that was about to jump out and eat us, but she never once jinked or tried to turn and run off. The railway tunnel that she finds scary is always "filled with Reiki light and energy" and we calmly walked through without fuss now.

I find that giving her 10 minutes or so Reiki before we leave the yard helps her relax, and it really does bring her down if adrenalin starts flowing, making it more of a pleasant ride/work time for both of us.

I also let her have a munch where the scary spots are, as you know, a lowered head is not on adrenalin and if able to eat, relaxes her much quicker... and next time it's not as scary or a bad place to be as the grass tastes sooo good!

Brenda Pullan

Scary objects

As we all know the list of scary objects we could encounter may go on for ever, so I'll put them all together under one heading!

When we meet something that the horse may decide to shy at, whether he's actually scared of it or not, we can use the same exercise.

We are simply going to put a golden or white light around the object, with the intent of making the object appealing, for example, if a horse I was training took a disliking to bin bags, I would think of golden light surrounding and encompassing the bag, whilst thinking "I wonder if there are some nice carrots in that bag, thinking of the horse crunching yummy carrots" – hence I am putting intent on the bin bag making it inviting!

When dealing with horses that have a tendency to shy at things, I like to try and stay one step ahead, so for instance, I keep an eye on what is ahead, anything that may give the horse an excuse to shy, will be covered in golden light and made inviting and interesting. At the same time, I am not focusing all my attention on these objects, the horse would find this strange and probably act up more, I see objects as I look around and within a second they are covered in golden light, then as we approach I am treating them as if they do not exist, they are too boring in my opinion to be given any attention to. I will look at something else completely, say watch the beauty of a bird in a field.

After just a few times of carrying out the above exercise we tend to see improvement in the horse, some people see improvement straight away, whilst others take a little longer, each case is individual and shouldn't be rushed.

If you are having a particular problem with an object, try sending Reiki to the situation, for example, I was having an issue with a bird scarer, which banged loudly just as we were passing on the horses. I wanted to take my young horse I had just backed on a hack, but to get to the good track we had to pass the bird scarer, so I sent Reiki to the situation, thinking that I would like to make it a nice enjoyable hack out for my youngster, free from loud banging objects. As I drove by the field the next morning, the bird scarer was gone! We went for a lovely hack! – Thank you Universe!

Scary places

If your horse becomes upset by the same place every time he hacks out, there is probably a bit of uneasy energy there. Sometimes this can be caused by something bad happening in a place, sometimes it can be a place where other horses have 'played up' and your horse senses that energy, what ever the reason for the energy change in that place we can simply neutralize it. You can do this distantly or whilst riding. I like to 'blast' the area with lots of white light, neutralizing the energy in that area. Some people like to use CKR for space clearance; you can choose what feels right for you to do at the time.

Scary traffic

It is always helpful to allow the horse to see traffic when he is relaxed with friends in the field. His friends show him the traffic is nothing to be afraid of and this is already conditioned for the horse when you take him out to see traffic on the road. Unfortunately this isn't always possible and sometimes even when the horse has been introduced to traffic in this way he may still become unsettled by large lorries or tractors.

Another exercise you can use is to follow the scary object around, so say if your horse is scared of tractors, see if you can borrow a tractor from someone, ask a friend to drive it around the field, nice and slowly, and ask the horse to follow the tractor. To start with the horse may not be too keen, but after a while, we can begin to put our intent on the situation, we begin to think of chasing the tractor, this becomes a game that the horse enjoys and he will get closer and closer to the tractor, chasing it around the field – tractor no longer scary!

When out hacking it is important to remember to breathe and visualize how we would like the horse to behave. To take things a step further we can use our intent, to put an energy bubble around the horse, which nothing can enter, see the horses energy bubble being stronger than that of the traffic. Look at where the line runs down the middle of the road, now imagine a barrier of energy along this line, this barrier of energy makes the horse feel safe in the space that he has.

Meeting other horses

Some horses can have quite an issue with meeting other horses whilst hacking. For some it is because they haven't met the horse before, whilst for others they want to join with the horse they meet.

When riding a stallion out you find that he would quite like to join every mare he meets! To help with this issue I imagine being surrounded by a bubble of golden light, within this bubble it is just the two of us, we are unaffected by any other goings on around us. This exercise can work very well and seems to build up potency the more you use it.

Not wanting to leave friends

It is only natural for the horse to want to stay with his herd. They are a herd animal and they like company. I don't see this as a problem, but instead a test. A test to see how fun I can make the horses work and how confident I can encourage him to be; if the horse enjoys his work and is confident in himself, he will happily go with you as his friend. You can be part of his herd, so he is not leaving on his own.

When we first start taking our horses away from the herd to further educate, we bring another horse with them, so if we are teaching them to be tied up on the yard we will use an older horse with a stable energy. We tie the older horse on the yard too and he creates a calm energy for the horse. If you haven't an older horse to use, you can create this same energy yourself, using your intent. Whilst the horse is tied up in the yard, we will brush him, finding out where he like to be brushed most and just focusing on that area. We may only keep him there for 5 minutes, giving him a lovely brush in his favourite place; then he is returned to his other friends. The horse goes away and thinks about it, he realises that spending time with a human is rather nice.

We can take this approach in other work too. So say we are taking a horse out down the road for the first time alone (after leading him out following another horse) we can give him nice scratches on his neck, we can take a few treats to change his brain to think of food if he seems upset, but most importantly we put our intent on our time. We think of our walk out with the horse as an adventure, something fun where we go exploring together. All too often owners will think of it as something scary or to be afraid of, the horse picks up on this and acts accordingly.

If you have an older horse with separation anxieties, you will already know that this has been conditioned to the horse, so instead of just learning something new like the above, we need to help to change something that the horse believes.

It is important to take things slowly. We can use an older horse again, so that when the horse is taken away from friends there is still another horse there, even though it is not her usual friend. This does help to calm the horse. Again we are looking to make the time enjoyable when the horse leaves the herd, lots of nice scratches and lots of praise for even the slightest bit of calmness. Visualising how the horse should behave will help too.

After a few times bringing the horse away from the herd, you will most likely find that she looks to you, this is great, however, you may find that whilst you are standing with her she is fine, however, if you need to walk away, she may start jumping all over the place! Again take things slowly. Stand by her whilst she is tied up and send Reiki to help calm her, emotionally and physically. Then perhaps go and sit down 15 feet away, let your attention still be with the horse, but have a set time that you will stay there for. The horse will pick up on the fact that you have a set time, so say you may like to drink a cup of tea, this seems to work better than just going and sitting away from the horse, as the horse realizes there is a timescale and you will be back on finishing what you are doing.

Hard to stop

First of all let me just say, my opinion is that if a horse is very hard to stop and is putting himself and rider in danger then you need to take preventative measures straight away.

When riding a horse that is becoming quite keen we can put up energy barriers. So if I am riding a horse that suddenly takes hold of the bit and becomes strong I will visualize a wave of water coming towards me, I think that the horse is cantering through the deep water, thus making it hard for him, it can be quite amazing just how much difference this exercise can achieve.

If a horse has become strong, one can imagine a cliff edge at the place they need to stop, this will give the rider more power to stop, as if you are trying to save an animal from running over a cliff, you bring up hidden strengths within you. These are always readily available; it is just simply learning to access them.

Lacking enthusiasm

Sometimes a horse may be slow because he doesn't want to leave his friends, whilst on other occasions it may be due to having a steady nature.

To help horses that are riding for a long distance or may be lacking in energy, we can think of energizing the horses body, This only takes ten seconds and you can do this as many times as you feel necessary whilst riding.

You are simply going to think of lots of energy, coming up from the earth, up into the horses hooves, up his legs, through his body, up his neck and to his head, this energy swirls throughout the horses body and brings energy to his step. You may like to try this exercise a few times before you are in the saddle, just to practice.

Jumping

When giving Reiki treatments to aid with jumping I would suggest not to give a full treatment just before the horse is due to jump, this is simply because it can make the horse a little too relaxed, he will most likely give a lovely round with a great rhythm and style, however you may find he doesn't think it is necessary to give that final push for the jump off.

Off putting jumps

Horses often have a particular type of jump that they are not so keen on, this may be the planks or perhaps the dreaded fillers. When we are riding a horse which is known to have a dislike for a particular type of jump we can use Reiki to help the issue. I tend to use these four stages:

1) Connect to Reiki and surround the jump in white light,
2) Put an inviting energy on the jump,
3) Visualize the horse jumping confidently over the jump,
4) Imagine how you will feel when the horse goes over the jump easily, how happy you will be, feel this feeling for a good few seconds.

The Golden Trail

As a child, I used to worry about forgetting my way around the course, that I would go wrong. To combat this feeling I would imagine a golden trail being laid down as I walked the course. Persons watching me jumping the course would always say, "it looks like the horse already knows where it is going", the truth is, she did know where she was going, she followed the trail I had laid down and did all the work for me.

Physical Energy Boost

Before I enter the jumping ring, I like to charge my horse with some positive Cho Ku Rei (CKR) energy to boost his physical energy and stamina. I will carry this out for just 2 – 5 minutes. Just simply draw the symbol, say the name three times and allow the energy to run through your body and into the horse.

Pronounced 'Show Koo Ray', this symbol represents Earth Ki.

The energy from Cho Ku Rei relates to our physical body and physical reality. It is often referred to as 'The Power Symbol' as it can feel very powerful, however this does not mean that this symbol is more powerful than the others, it's energy is just different and perhaps more apparent as it is related to the physical body and we feel things with our physical body. Draw the symbol in your minds eye. Some people prefer to draw the symbol in violet as this is the colour mostly associated with Reiki energy, however, it doesn't matter whether the symbol is drawn in violet or just with light; it will still work. After drawing the symbol, say the symbols name silently to yourself three times. The combination of drawing the symbol and saying the symbols name three times 'activates' the symbol and produces its effects.

Drawing Instructions for Cho Ku Rei

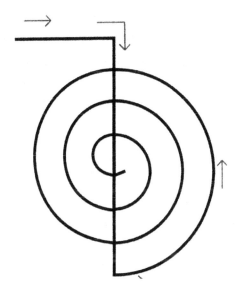

Knocking poles

If a horse suddenly starts knocking poles for no apparent reason I would have his back checked.

Some horses will knock the first fence, due to concentration, or tend to knock the upright fences or loose enthusiasm and begin to knock fences part way round the course. If this is the case, I would use lots of visualization, imagining the horse picking his feet up well, really tucking them out of the way. You may like to go one step further and think of the horse jumping higher than is needed for the jump.

It can also be helpful to work over simple poles at home, perhaps putting some doubles up, just to help the horse with his jumping skills. We often find that horses jump better over solid fences, so you may like to practice over some small cross country fences.

Excitement

The most common problem I hear from jumpers is that the horse becomes over excited when he sees the jumps, this means the horse will use up much more energy than he actually needs, it may affect his concentration and quite often the rider does not feel at ease!

In these circumstances, it is helpful to give a Reiki treatment the day before the competition. Whilst giving the treatment we can visualise how we would like the horse to behave when he sees the jumps.

When you arrive at the competition, just spend a couple of minutes giving Reiki to the horse thinking of the same visualization. This can be done whilst the horse is still in the horse box if it is easier.

Dressage

There are many ideals associated with dressage, many people become stuck, focusing on the head being in with an arched neck, instead of focusing on engaging the hind quarters so that the horse naturally carries himself.

To improve the over all dressage experience I would suggest watching a person you admire riding. Nuno Oliverio is a good choice. Watch and admire and then imagine yourself looking the same on your own horse. Just watching a good rider and horse will help to improve your riding as your subconscious will take in everything you see and make it easier for you to achieve.

Schooling at home: Slaying 'Monsters' with Reiki Symbols

By Elinor Mary Thomas

"The Indoor Arena is a <u>very</u> dangerous place. Invisible Monsters lurk in the far corners and they are so big that they make the whole place creak, groan, clatter and clang every time they 'breathe'. Even the roof makes sudden loud scraping noises and the 'monsters' howl and cry – these are truly terrifying sounds. I stay on full alert, ready to take flight at all times and ensure that I keep Mum and myself safe by staying well away from the far end. If Mum tries to ride me in that direction I do a swift about turn and shoot back to the slightly safer end as fast as possible. I don't understand why she doesn't appreciate this." (My horse's side of the story!)

This is true. One winter nearly all our schooling sessions took place in the 'A' end of the arena! It <u>is</u> a creaky building and when it is windy the trees and bushes scrape their branches on the metal sides and really do make the most spine-chilling noises. When the two large sliding doors move they give an impression of rolling thunder that would be appropriate for a horror film sound-track. Yes, the horse was understandably scared, but her sudden reactions of bolting/bucking scared me!

So … before mounting I started leading my horse round the whole arena, stopping in each corner to connect to Reiki and to draw massive symbols (CKR or SHK - whichever felt 'right' on that day) in the air. If anyone else was sharing the arena I did this silently in my head (for obvious reasons!), otherwise I was happy to say the name of the symbol out loud whilst drawing the shapes with large sweeping gestures.

Once mounted, I rode round and visualised the symbols (floor to roof size and about a metre thick) at the school letters A, E, C, and B. At each letter I imagined taking in the energy from the symbol as we rode through it. Then we would change the rein up the centre line. At letter X we rode the shape of a huge CKR, continued up the centre line, then I visualised the symbols at letters H, K, F and M and rode 'through' them. I would 'chant' the Kotodoma of whichever symbol I had used. (Note : I find these symbols quite powerful and before trying this I would advise checking that the horse is used to experiencing Reiki energy.)

This routine was not an instant success, but by degrees, we were able to venture closer to letter 'C' and now I am pleased to say that we use the whole arena and I only resort to the leading round and the symbol-drawing on the very worst windy days! (Maybe that's more for me than my horse!)

Elinor Mary Thomas
www.sofarsogoodtherapy.co.uk

Forgetting the test

We can use the same exercise in dressage as we did in the jumping. Simply imagine a golden trail being plotted out on the dressage arena; you may like to imagine darker patches where transitions are. This not only helps the horse know where he is going, but it will also be picked up by your body as you ride around. You can also visualize each part of the test, imagining how the horse will look through each transition and movement.

Dressage arena nightmares

There are a few 'nightmares' in the dressage arena, firstly we have to walk into an area where the walls are covered with brightly coloured advertisements, then comes the white boards, the judges box, not to mention those scary flower boxes!

You can either work with all these objects as a whole or with each one individually. Take your time, connect to Reiki and spread beautiful white light right around the dressage arena, see the light gently swirling around any 'scary' objects, making them appealing to the horse.

Staying in the arena

This can pose a problem, especially for the inexperienced dressage horse, and although it can be fun to watch, it's not so fun to be the rider!

To help keep the horse inside the dressage boards, we can make an energy barrier, it is probably easiest to do this when dismounted but with practice you will find that you are able to achieve the same outcome whilst riding.

1) Connect to Reiki
2) Visualize the dressage arena in your minds eye
3) Now focus or 'zoom in' on the dressage borders.
4) Imagine making these borders taller, so that they are more like a fence than a small board
5) See them being strong

6) Imagine the horse staying within the boards whilst you are riding him

7) Feel how happy you are when the horse has stayed in the arena; focus on this feeling for a few seconds.

Relaxation, rhythm and impulsion

These are very common factors in which marks are lost. We can use the same exercise with each of the above to help enhance the horses over all way of going.

To do this simply connect to Reiki and think of what you would like, for example, if I was riding a horse and would like more impulsion, I would stand or walk whilst mounted, put my hand on the horses wither, connect to Reiki and say 'more impulsion', I would allow the energy and intent to flow into the horse for a couple of minutes and then carry on warming up.

Movements

For all movements we can visualize where the horses hooves are going to make contact with the ground, so say for instance we are looking to stand square, we will think of the horses hooves in this position, thinking of each hoof connected to the earth below, this in turn helps to make the horse stand still.

If you were going to imagine half-pass you may like to visualize the movement first and then imagine where the horses feet will land, imagine golden hoof prints where the horse will tread as he carries out his half-pass.

In the warm up

Often the warm up area can have more issues than the actual class we may be entering. We have lots to contend with, new/ excited/ nervous horses, a new area and frustrated humans, which means the warm up area isn't usually a very nice atmosphere for the horse.

Affected by other horses

If your horse is becoming upset by other horses in the ring we can put a bubble around him, where he is safe and secure. Sometimes other competitors don't show the courtesy they should and may ride too close upsetting your horse.

As you ride around think of being encased in a lovely bubble of light, the bubble stretches right around you and the horse creating a safe place, no one else can enter this space, it is just you and the horse together. Imagine that all of the other competitors have disappeared; it is just you and the horse.

Doesn't want to leave the warm up area

Sometimes the horse would prefer to stay in the warm up area with the other horses, rather than leave and complete his individual show. I like to use a mixture of visualization and intent to help the horse. I visualize the horse leaving the warm up ring easily and with a calm energy and I use my intent to make the entrance to the competition ring inviting, so that the horse wants to enter.

Rider becoming stressed

This is something that we see a lot of, not only at shows, but also in everyday working of horses. This simplest way to aid with this issue is through the use of the symbol Sei He Ki.

Pronounced 'Say Hay Key', this symbol represents Heavenly Ki.

The energy produced from Sei He Ki relates to us in a mental, emotional and spiritual way. This is the energy of our spiritual essence and brings harmony and balance to the mental and emotional aspects of ones self – and also the horse one is riding

Drawing Instructions for Sei He Ki

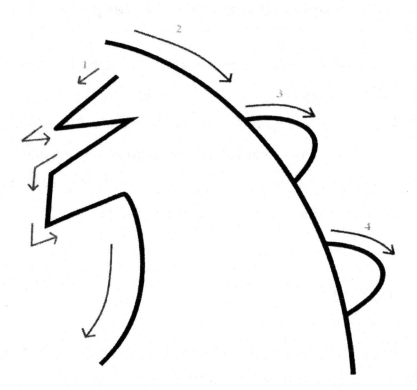

The left part of the symbol is drawn first (from top to bottom), then the right part (from top to bottom) and finally the two half circles (again from top to bottom).

We can use SHK for the horse and rider at the same time, I tend to always treat both at the same time, as even if it seems that just one of the pair is becoming stressed, the tension will affect both.

1) Connect to Reiki
2) Let your attention be placed on the horse and rider
3) Imagine drawing a lovely big SHK symbol above the riders head.
4) Say the symbols name three times to empower it
5) Allow the energy of SHK to flood over the rider and horse, like a waterfall of golden light flooding down over horse and rider.

You can also use this exercise for yourself whilst riding; just imagine the SHK symbol above you, say the name three times and enjoy the energy. If you find it hard to concentrate whilst doing Reiki on horseback, you could send the SHK symbol in advance, just like sending distant healing, with the intent that it will 'switch on' when you mount the horse.

Showing

After waking up at 5am to bath your horse, you've somehow managed to keep him clean, get yourself dressed into your best gear and be loaded on to the horsebox, hopefully on time.

Now the fun begins, on arriving at the show, said horse needs to be preened and polished at the same time as his rider. He needs to stand perfectly still and mannered during the line up, yet then come out and strut his stuff when gestured to.

Standing still

This can be particularly hard with a youngster, or inexperienced horse. The key is to practice at home with other horses next to us. We also need to remember to speak our truth, if you take an inexperienced horse into a show ring and the person next to you is allowing their horse to come too close, you need to ask them to keep their distance. So much training and trust can be lost, when we do not listen to our horse and speak out when needed to.

If your horse is fidgeting, the following meditation can be very useful

1) Look at the horses body allowing your eyes to soften

2) Let your attention drift down to the horses hooves

3) See the connection each hoof has with the ground below

4) Imagine that the hoof and leg is actually a tree trunk, imagine roots coming from the hooves and stretching down into the ground below.

5) The roots bring the calmness of the earth to the being of the horse

Calling out

When the horse is doing something undesirable, we have to make sure that we do not focus lots of attention on this behaviour – the more attention we give the unwanted behaviour the more power we give to it.

Instead, we simply think of the horse being completely normal, for example, in the case of calling out in a show ground, we just think of the horse being happy and quiet, enjoying his time at the show, feeling secure with his owner and happy to stand around in a calm atmosphere.

Showing off

When your turn to strut your stuff finally comes round, more often than not you will have been standing still for at least five to ten minutes, or a lot longer. The horse switches off and would rather be asleep!

My favourite trick for show classes is to use the CKR symbol on the horse I am riding, a couple of minutes before it is our turn.

You could either draw CKR above yourself and the horse, say it's name three time and allow the energy to cascade over you both, energizing the horse (and rider!)

Or you could imagine an energizing light spreading through the horses body, awakening the muscles and brain.

Further techniques

Sometimes there is a certain factor that will set a horse into a different mind set whilst at a show or in everyday life. The meditation we will be discussing shortly is very useful for horses that are having a reaction to a particular circumstance; this could include anything from reacting badly to the start bell in the competition ring or 'freaking out' in narrow/ small spaces or running from dogs

By feeling what the horse is feeling in the situation we can have a greater understanding of what his body feels before he reacts and then send Reiki to the parts of his body which make him react in that way. This meditation is as easy to complete distantly as it is in the company of the horse;

Meditation to 'become' the horse;

1) Close your eyes, take a few deep breathes,
2) Clear your mind, let all thoughts float away
3) Connect to Reiki
4) Feel your body begin to glow with the build up of energy, allow the energy to shine from every part of your body.
5) Carry on letting your body emit beautiful, calm, loving energy for around 5 - 10 minutes
6) When you feel ready ask the horses permission to feel what he is feeling, to spiritually enter his physical self
7) Now imagine an energy within you, a light wispy energy, rise up through your body and out through your crown
8) Let this energy go to the horses crown chakra and then down in to his body
9) As the energy enters the horses body it gradually expands

10) As the energy fills the horses body, your body becomes the horses body, you are inside the horse, let your self expand to his shape, your legs become his legs, your body becomes his body, your arms become his forearms, your neck becomes his neck, your head becomes his head.

11) Take note of how you feel inside the horse, physically and emotionally

12) Now visualize the horse at say, the competition arena, you are still there inside the horse feeling how it feels to walk on his feet, feeling how his rider sits on his back

13) Become very aware of the feelings you may now receive in your body and listen to the competition 'start bell' ring or buzz

14) Feel what this does to the horse, how it makes him feel, how loud it sounds, how his body consequently reacts and how his rider then reacts to him

15) Once you have felt this we can then go on to treat the areas that are needed, so say in this case, before the bell went off, the horse could feel his riders anticipation, which made him ready to react, the sound of the bell to the horse sounded like an aeroplane flying over rather than just a bell, the horses heart was pounding, his blood rushing, he had to react in some way and jumping 4 foot in the air seemed the right thing to do.

16) The next step is to send Reiki to each of the feelings the horse had, whilst still in his body, so we go back to the competition arena, we already know when, where and why the horse is going to react so we can send Reiki before; as the rider tenses we send Reiki through the horses back , to the points he feels the tensions through, we then send Reiki to the issue of the bell, we send Reiki to 'block out' how loud the bell seems, we think of enjoying the sound the of the bell right through our body, as the bell sounds Reiki will already be flowing around the heart and body to keep things even, feel yourself breathing deeply relaxing your body. You may have to go through this process 3 or 4 times in a row before the horses body feels completely calm throughout the whole process. Just gently carry on until he feels calm and able to cope with the situation without his body reacting severely.

17) When you are ready to finish the treatment, thank the horse and then gently leave his body, see the wispy energy leave through his poll area and come back in to you through your crown

Example

I had been asked to treat a friends' horse, which she had recently bought who had an issue with narrow gaps, for example, walking through gateways and stable doors. I carried out the

exercise above and 'became' the horse as he went through a narrow gateway. I could feel that he was ready for the gate to bang into him and then I saw a picture of a gate hitting him, perhaps being blown in the wind, I also had the feeling that this had happened quite a lot of times. I sent Reiki to the situation and also sent Reiki to the area around the gates on the premises and his stable door. When I had finished the treatment I told his owner what I had felt, she hadn't thought of this and was presuming he was being naughty, as his last owners were very inexperienced and she thought he had learnt to walk all over them. After the treatment the horse had improved a lot, staying a lot calmer whilst moving through gateways and his owner was a lot happier too, as she felt that she understood him more and treated him with patience instead of becoming cross.
Sue

It may be hard when first practicing this exercise to remember exactly what to do, however, the process is not set in stone, our aim is to 'become' the horse in his stressful situation and help him to a higher degree, so just practising to become the horse without going to the stressful situation is a good idea.

The above exercise is also very useful to help determine problems we may be having at home, if we feel that our horse 'isn't quite right in his canter' say, we can 'feel' what he feels whilst cantering.

The Aura

Every living thing has an electromagnetic field or aura around it. The aura is made of energy, someone may have a very positive aura, say for instance when you meet someone and you instantly take a like to them, knowing that they are a lovely person. Or a person may have a negative aura, the space around them being filled with all of the negative energy they create; this could be typical of someone who loves saying horrible things about people, once again, you may sense this about a person as soon as you lay your eyes on them.

Some people may start of sensing auras and then after a time, when they least expect it they will suddenly see someone's aura. Don't worry if you don't see colours straight away, for a while some persons can see an energy or mist and gradually after a time the colours come in to view.

First we need to focus on 'feeling the aura'. Most of you will already have felt the aura around a human or animal, it is the energy they are portraying and 'putting out' and so also the energy that they will attract towards themselves. Take some time now to see what your aura is portraying:

1) Close your eyes and take a few deep breathes
2) Clear your mind, let any thoughts you are having gently float away
3) Now let your attention fall to your aura; does the energy around you feel bright and strong? Does the energy around you feel down and swamped?
4) Write down what you feel.

Example

Whilst carrying out the feeling your own aura exercise I first became aware of the energy around my head feeling light, I then became very aware of the energy around my Tanden being very strong and powerful

Sue

I liked this exercise; it made me more aware of the state of my aura in everyday life. I close my eyes and focus on the energy surrounding me; sometimes I will see or feel an area which is a bit depleted. I then send Reiki to my aura, so that it shines brightly in all directions. I have noticed the difference when I charge my aura; I have more energy and seem to have a better day!

Helen

It may take a few times to get to grips with this exercise, but if you just practice for a couple of minutes each day for 3 or 4 days, you will begin to feel your aura and become more aware of when you may need to send Reiki to yourself. You will begin to sense when your aura is feeling low and in turn be able to make it stronger and give your body any help it may need. It is important when treating animals to keep our energy and aura in a stable, loving condition. Horses read our aura and the energy within us the moment they meet us, so to show that we are loving and have nice relaxing yet strong energy is an important aspect as to how the horse will accept us and want to share energy with us.

To begin sensing or feeling the horse's aura we use pretty much the same exercise as sensing your own:

1) Close your eyes and take a few deep breathes
2) Clear your mind, let any thoughts gently drift away
3) Now let your attention focus on the energy around the horse. Looking in your minds eye, see where the aura is strong, see

where the aura is depleted and closer to the body. Feel whether the energy is calm or whether the energy is dancing around all over the place. At this stage some people may see colours and some will see just a haze of energy.

Example

When I started this exercise I could see a haze of energy around the horse through my third eye. The energy was closer to the horse around his hindquarters, so I began to send Reiki to the horses aura. As I was sending Reiki I began to see a dull/faded red over the hindquarters, the red became brighter and began to shine as I sent Reiki to that area.

Emma Stokes

On connecting with my horse I could feel her energy was very erratic. After just a few minutes of sending Reiki I could feel her energy calm and she began to relax.

Sue

Again this may take a few attempts before you start feeling the aura, but don't give up, take your time and just 'have a go'! It is the use of your intent that is important here; just the same as when you ask to see the chakras.

The next exercise we can try is to physically feel the aura, some of you may have done this already; whilst scanning. The practitioner will usually hold their hand(s) slightly away from the horse, they will usually find that the place where they have chosen to scan is actually on a layer of the aura, so Reiki people tend to do this anyway, even without knowing it

To feel the aura with your hand:

1) Stand next to the horse, take a few deep breathes and centre yourself.

2) Keep your eyes slightly open so that you can watch where your hand gravitates

3) Hold your hand approx ½ meter away from the horses shoulder/ wither area.

4) Let your hand slowly, softly drop down closer to the horse, be aware of any feelings in your hand, a magnetic pull or a slight resistance, the same sort of feeling as if you are holding a ball of energy between your hands.

5) When you feel that you have felt the edge of the aura, slowly and gently let your hand float along the back of the horse, be aware if your hand feels it can suddenly go closer to the horse, this would indicate an area where the aura is depleted.

You will most likely need to practice the exercises above a good few times before moving onto the exercise below; calming the horses' aura. Practicing the exercises above will make you ready to calm a horses aura in a very short amount of time. It is an invaluable aid to be able to calm a horse quickly in any situation, especially when working with horses that are highly strung and very excitable.

The exercise below is appropriate when a horse's aura needs to be calmed;

1) Take a few deep breathes and centre yourself.

2) Feel energy coming down through your crown, into your Tanden and building in your hand. This energy is calming, soothing, yet strong.

3) Approach the horse; let him sniff the energy in your hand.

4) Now, as you breathe out stroke down the aura on the horses neck, a long sweeping stroke, perhaps 3 to 4 times, feeling the horse connect to your calm strong energy, letting the horse connect to you and resonate at the same energy that you are portraying.

Example

I tried this exercise on my horse when I took him to a competition, he was rather excited and to be honest I wasn't sure if it would work. I took some deep breaths, felt the energy in my hand and stroked his aura, down his neck, as I breathed out, he looked at me took a huge sigh and relaxed!

Helen Berry

A mare we had in for stud was becoming stressed in the stable; she had only arrived a few hours beforehand and was quite highly strung. I tried the above exercise on her, at first she had no response whatsoever, I carried on and when I stroked her aura for the 5th time she exhaled in time with me and relaxed her muscles and body

Again don't worry if you find this hard at first, you don't have to have a horse that is excitable to practice on, just trying the exercises a few times over will begin to sow the seed and allow you to connect, feel and see the horses' aura.

Some horses may appear to be calm and settled when really their aura is all over the place, changing from minute to minute, these types of horses are often very depressed and have lost or are losing touch with what their energy is doing. This can be quite deliberate. Perhaps a better way to explain this is that these types of horses are becoming more 'human' in the way they control or ignore what their energy is doing. The more we share energy with this type of horse, the more horse like he will become.

Colours: what could they mean?

After a time you may begin to see colours within the aura whilst looking through your minds eye, this is not essential but can give further clarification to an issue. You may also find that after seeing colours in the aura in your minds eye you may gradually begin to see the colours of the aura with your eyes open, this may first occur when you see someone with strong emotions, say you see someone who is very annoyed and see a glow of red around the part of their body where they are holding the anger. As this develops further you may find that you can see auras and their colours whenever you want to.

In general, the more colourful, cleaner and brighter the aura and the more constant the energy distribution in the aura, the healthier and more balanced the horse is; just as when we work with the chakras.

We are each unique individuals and colors may hold different meanings for us than for others, just as a piece of music inspires different feelings in different people. So although there may be many similarities in what a certain colour may mean, it is most important for you to feel what that colour means to you in the way in which it is being portrayed. Different tones of the same color communicate different meanings.

The colors of the horses' aura are also affected by the energies of other people. It is common for horses to have their owners' colors in their aura. You may suddenly get a feeling that this is not the horses own energy but that it has latched on to the horse via his owner or someone else close to him.

The aura can contain any one of the million colour variations in the universe. So it is best to try not to put the colours into a definitive category. There are some generalised themes which can help us to interpret what a colour could mean. It is most important though for you to feel what that colour means to you, let your intuition guide you as to what you feel that colour represents. These are some rough guidelines for interpreting the colour of the aura;

Red

Red can symbolize; passion, energy, strength, physical activity, courage creativity, warmth, and security. It can also be associated with aggression. Seeing red in the aura can signify materialism, materialistic ambition, a focus on sensual pleasures, a quick temper, survival, raw passion, anger, frustration, menstruation, determination, sense of importance and feeling overwhelmed by change

Orange

Orange can symbolize the individual's relationship to the external world, the needs and wants of the physical body and the ways in which these are satisfied. In the aura orange can signify thoughtfulness and creativity, sensuality, physical pleasure, emotional self-expression, creativity, lacking reason, lacking self-discipline, health and vitality

Yellow

Yellow symbolizes intellect, creativity, happiness and the power of persuasion. In the aura yellow may signify intellectual development; for either material or spiritual ends, mental alertness, analytical thought, happiness, optimism, child-like, ego driven and thinking at expense of feeling

Green

Green symbolizes money, luck, prosperity, vitality and fertility. It is also associated with envy. In the aura green can signify balance, peace and often indicates ability as a healer, peace, nurturing, new growth, fear, need for security, jealousy, envy and balance

Blue

Blue is the color of spirituality, intuition, inspiration and inner peace. It is also associated with sadness and depression (the "blues"). In the aura blue can indicate serenity, contentment and spiritual development, verbal communication, freethinking, relating to structure and organization, emphasis on business, male energies, sadness and possibilities

Indigo

Indigo is associated with psychic ability. In the aura indigo can indicate a seeker, often of spiritual truth.

Purple

Purple is associated with power, both earthly and spiritual. In the aura purple may signify higher spiritual development, wisdom, authoritative, female energies, matriarchal, sense of superiority, controlling, imagination and intuition

White

White is associated with truth, purity, cleansing, healing and protection. In the aura it can signify a high level of attainment, a higher level soul incarnate to help others, very high spiritual vibration, godly, divine, inspiration, seeing spiritual big picture and compassionate

White – cloudy

New Age or religious energy, lacking consciousness, a cover-up, denial, being 'good' at expense of being 'whole'

Gold

Gold represents understanding and luck. Remember though that nothing comes from nothing. In the aura it can represent service to others, high spiritual vibration, integrity, respect, freedom, clear seeing, integrating spirit and body, creating as spirit

Pink

Pink represents unconditional love, love requiring nothing in return. It is also the color of friendship and conviviality. In the aura it can signify balance between the spiritual and the material, self-love, tenderness, female energies, gay energies, emphasis on physical appearances, being 'nice' at expense of being 'real'

Brown

Brown is the color of the earth and represents practicality, material success, concentration and study. In the aura it can indicate "down to earth-ness" and common sense, grounding, practical, male energies, invalidating, emphasizing body and denying spirit, feeling worth-less

Black

Black is the absence of color. It represents the unconscious and mystery. In the aura it can signify some kind of blockage or something being hidden, issues relating to death, hatred, lack of forgiveness, unresolved karma, dark intentions, shadow games, needing compassion for self

Riders

Improving Position

Our position affects how the horse can move underneath us. If we are tipping our body forwards we are impeding the movement of the shoulders. If we are leaning the weight backwards, we become behind the movement and this is usually accompanied by 'pushing' the horse with the seat.

Where tension is apparent in the body, this in turn will cause tension in other parts of the body, for example, if we are not supple through our hips this will cause tension in the legs, often shown by heels being raised or knees gripping.

Being supple and free is something that we should work on continuously, I would highly recommend yoga classes for all persons who horse ride, in the world today we are very lucky, just being able to turn on the television and pick up channels where we can follow along with yoga exercises. We don't need to do this for hours each day, even 10 minutes of your day will make a huge difference. Can you spare 10 minutes? 10 minutes to make you feel better on your horse, better in yourself and improve the way of going in yourself and your horse.

When sitting on the horse it can be very helpful to think of the 3 point seat. Your seat bones make 2 points, the third point is the coccyx, which although not in contact with the saddle, can be thought of as joining down through the seat. We should think of equal pressure being put on each of these points, as we sit quietly on the horse.

A visualisation technique to aid the position:

Imagine a white light of energy running along your spine from the Coccyx, right the way up the spine to the neck and up to the crown on top of the head. This energetic channel or route reaches from the sky above you and runs right through your body. This channel connects you to the upper realms of thinking clearly and being spiritually aware whilst riding.

The white energy line also runs from your coccyx, through the horse and joins to the ground, this is your grounding whilst riding, it gives stability and strength. It is the balance of the pelvis and security of the legs.

The crown joins your body to the world above you, leading vertically upwards, you can feel your body lift as you think of the energy connection. Your chest opens as the gentle pull of energy reaches from your crown above. This gives you the ability to think clearly whilst riding and supports the balance of the upper body.

State of mind – rider

The riders' state of mind is one of the most important factors for a happy horse. We need to be in the now, not thinking of chores to do, disagreements or what others may be thinking of us. To the horse this would create very mixed messages, as we are sending him these messages through energy, and quite frankly, what does he care about the washing up! All it means to him, is that you are not together at that time, you are else where and he is like a robot working for someone without understanding of his needs.

Whilst riding I like to stay very much with my horses in my mind, we work through visualisation and communicate through energy and thought.

A few years ago I was helping with a horse who was quite a professional in the 'bucking/ rodeo style'. This horse could really put on a show.

Later that day, I was riding my bombproof gelding, who is a real rock steady eddy, as we were just having a warm up, the bucking horse came into my mind, I began to think of the bucks and wondered if I would still be able to stay on something like that – I am getting older!

I then asked my horse to go into canter and he gave me exactly what I had been telling him about, a series of rather large bucks – so you see my horses like to keep me in line and focused on the task at hand; enjoyment of riding.

If you find it hard to shut out the world whilst riding, send yourself Reiki for this issue, you could do this distantly the evening before riding.

For persons who have a lot on their minds I suggest to give themselves around ten minutes before riding, to sit down and carry out Hatsurei:

    1) Relax:

Relax and close your eyes, and place your hands palms down on your lap.

Focus your attention on your Dantien point: an energy centre two fingerbreadths (3-5 cm) below your tummy button and 1/3 of the way into your body.

2) Mokunen (Focusing)

Say to yourself "I'm going to start Hatsu Rei now".

3) Kenyoku

This means 'Dry Bathing' or 'Brushing Off'

Kenyoku can be seen as a way of getting rid of negative energy. It has correspondences with Taoist massage, or meridian massage. Here is what to do

Place the fingertips of your right hand near the top of the left shoulder, where the collarbone meets the bulge of the shoulder. The hand is lying flat on your chest.

Draw your flat hand down and across the chest in a straight line, over the base of the sternum (where your breastbone stops and your abdomen starts, in the midline) and down to the right hip. Exhale as you do this.

Do the same on the right side, using your left hand. Draw your left hand from the right shoulder, in a straight line across the sternum, to the left hip, and again exhale as you make the downward movement

Do the same on the left side again (like you did at the start), so you will have carried out movements with your right hand, left hand, and right hand again.

Now put your right fingertips on the outer edge of the left shoulder, at the top of your slightly outstretched left arm, with your fingertips pointing sideways away from your body.

Move your right hand, flattened, along the outside of your arm, Keep the hand moving all the way to the fingertips and beyond, all the while keeping the left arm straight. Exhale as you do this. Repeat this process on the right side, with the left hand placed on the right shoulder, and move it down the right arm to the fingertips and beyond. Exhale as you do this.

Repeat the process on the left side again, so you will have carried out movements with your right hand, left hand, and right hand again, like before.

4) Connect to Reiki

Raise your hands high up in the air on either side of your head, with your palms facing the sky and your fingers pointing towards the midline. Connect to Reiki by visualising energy or white light cascading into your hands and running through your arms into your body. Feel the sensations. As you become aware of Reiki flowing, slowly lower your hands. This position is the first of the "Eight Brocades" in QiGong: connecting heaven and earth.

5) Joshin Kokkyu Ho

This means "Technique for Purification of the Spirit" or "Soul Cleansing Breathing Method". This is a meditation that focuses on the Dantien point

Put your hands on your lap with your palms facing upwards and breathe naturally through your nose. Focus on your Dantien point and relax

When you breathe in, visualise energy or light flooding into your crown chakra and passing into your Dantien and, as you pause before exhaling, feel that energy expand throughout your body, melting all your tensions.

When you breathe out, imagine that the energy floods out of your body in all directions as far as infinity.

You should soon feel energy/tingling in your hands and even in your feet, as the meditation progresses!

6) Gassho

Gassho means "hands together", and the correct position to hold is to have your hands together in front of your chest (like praying hands) a little higher that your heart, so that you could breathe out onto your fingertips if you wanted to.

Hold this position for meditation.

An important aspect of this meditation is that you should focus your awareness on the point where your middle fingers touch. You might try putting your tongue up to touch the roof of your mouth with each in-breath, and release the tongue on each out-breath, and see if this makes any difference to your experience of this stage.

7) Seishin Toitsu

This means "my mind is focused" or "my spirit is gathered", and is the stage when Reiju is given by teachers in the Gakkai.

Stay in the Gassho position.

When you breathe in, visualise energy or light flooding into your hands and passing into your Dantien: breathe in through your hands.

Feel the energy accumulating and building there

When you breathe out, visualise that the energy stored in your Dantien floods out through your hands.

8) Gokai Sansho

Say the 5 Principles aloud, three times.

Just for today:

Do not anger

Do not worry

Be humble

Be honest

Be compassionate towards yourself and others

9) Mokunen

Put your hands back on to your laps with your palms down.

Say to yourself "I've finished Hatsu Rei Ho now" to your sub-conscious.

Hatsurei not only helps the state of mind, it helps the development of Reiki and using energy, so by using Hatsurei before riding, you will probably find that you feel a deeper connection with the energy if you need it whilst in the saddle.

Nervous Riders: Riding with confidence

Riding with confidence is something a lot of people find hard. There are always situations that may challenge us, but being brave isn't being without fear, being brave is learning to recognise the fear, accept the fear and master your fear.

Relaxation Exercise

The following exercise can make a real difference to your day, by just spending a few minutes in the morning relaxing all of your muscles; it lets the energy move freely around your body aiding positive thinking and feeling.

This exercise is one that is very helpful to use whilst riding; use it before you get on your horse and then again when you first get on. Going through each muscle group, making sure you aren't emanating any unnecessary tension through your muscles.

NB – for readers who have trouble sleeping at night, try this exercise – it can work wonders!

1) Sit or stand comfortably, let your body relax.

2) Take a few deep breathes. As you breathe in completely fill your lungs with air. As you breathe out feel your body relax.

3) Now we are going to go through your body from head to toe, gently relaxing your muscles and letting tension flow away. As you breathe in tense your muscles, hold the tension and then as you breathe out let your muscles relax down and let any tension flow away.

4) Starting with your head and facial muscles; breathe in and tense your forehead and jaw muscles, hold the tension for a few seconds and as you breathe out let your head and facial muscles relax.

5) Now, as you breathe in, tense your shoulders up, hold the tension for a few seconds, and then as you breathe out let your shoulders relax down, all of the tension from your shoulders and the top of your spine is gently released.

6) Breathe in and tense your arms, hands and wrists, feel the muscles tighten more and more and then when your ready breathe out and let your arms relax down, wobble your elbows.

7) Now, breathe in and tense your torso area, hold the muscles for a few seconds and as you breathe out let your tummy and lower back muscles relax.

8) Breathe in and tense your buttock and thigh muscles, hold the tension for a few seconds and then as you breathe out let them relax down, feeling comfortable.

9) Breathe in and tense your calves, ankles and feet, keep the tension for a couple of seconds and then as you breathe out let them softly relax down.

10) Now just go back through your body. Check how your neck and head are feeling; perhaps gently move your head from side to side. Check that your shoulders are feeling relaxed; softly roll them backwards two or three times. Check your arms are free from tension; gently wobble your elbows and then your wrists. Check your waist and legs are feeling relaxed; be aware of how they are softly hanging from your body.

Creating a Trigger response

When our body and mind are feeling nervous or afraid, obviously we are not in a good state physically or emotionally to try to have a successful horse riding session. The following exercise is very useful in that we can train our bodies to think of happy or positive thoughts.

1)   Think of a situation, place, animal, or person that makes you smile; like hearing a robin chirping to the midday sun, or spring blossoming; the buds on the trees beginning to bloom.

2)   Write a list of all the things that make you smile, that make you happy; remember they can be simple things, like a nice cup of tea in the morning! You may wish to add to the list over the span of a couple of days.

3)   Once your list has 10 subjects listed. I would like you to press your thumb to your middle finger on both hands, whilst at he same time reading down the list of things that make you smile, make sure as you read the list that you visualise each subject, feel how it makes you feel, so that you properly connect to it.

Pressing your thumb and middle finger together and thinking of happy thoughts will cause a stimulus response. After a few times of carrying out the exercise above, you will be able to press your thumb and middle finger together and your body will begin to 'feel' happy.

This means that whilst you are riding your horse you can press your thumb and middle finger together; which will cause an automatic response through your body and mind to feel happy, which in turn will help you to feel more confident and allow anxiety to dissolve.

Visualisation Exercise

Visualisation is an important tool not only in horse riding but also in life. Visualising how you will react to a situation will begin to train your body and mind how you wish it to react, putting you in control.

1)   Find somewhere quiet to sit where you won't be disturbed.

2)   Make yourself comfortable

3)   Close your eyes and take three deep breaths, in and out; feel the oxygen filling your lungs, and feel your body relax further as you breathe out.

4)   Let your mind become clear, if any images come into your mind just gently usher them away.

5)   Practice just relaxing and keeping your mind clear for a few minutes.

6)   Visualise yourself grooming your horse, putting his tack on, leading him to the mounting area. Now see yourself getting on your horse and riding.

7)   See yourself walking around on your horse, perhaps doing some circles and changes of rein. Be aware of how your body feels; see yourself relaxed and happy, riding with confidence.

8)   Now proceed to working trot; ride some 20m circles, perhaps a figure of 8 and any other school movement you wish; see yourself relaxed and happy, riding with confidence.

9)   Proceed to canter; again ride some 20m circles and change the rein. See yourself relaxed and happy, riding with confidence.

Don't worry if you find it hard to visualise at first; this will become easier with practice. Once you feel confident using this exercise you can tailor make it to fit the area where you need more confidence; for example, if you have worries regarding going into canter, you can visualise the canter transition and riding in canter over and over again, in all places in the arena. Or you may have worries regarding mounting your horse; if this is so you can visualise yourself mounting over and over again.

If your horse is spooky, bucks or naps you can visualise how you will cope with the situation; sitting up and keeping calm.

Begin to use visualisation in your everyday life; where thought goes energy flows.

Breathing Exercise

It is important that we breathe correctly whilst riding and in everyday life; poor breathing robs energy and negatively affects mental alertness. The rib cage and surrounding muscles get stiff causing inhalation to become more difficult. Less elasticity and weak muscles leave stale air in the tissues of the lungs and prevents fresh oxygen from reaching the blood stream.

The following exercise is a simple way to deepen breathing and to cleanse the lungs. This exercise will also increase energy and decrease tension.

1) Lie flat on your back to get a proper sense of deep breathing. (Have some small pillows available to reduce strain by tucking them under the neck and knees. The natural course of breathing in that position will create a slight rise in the stomach upon inhaling and a slight fall upon exhaling.)

2) Place your hands on your stomach, palms down, at the base of the rib cage, middle fingers barely touching each other, and take a slow deep breath. As the diaphragm pushes down, the stomach will slightly expand causing the fingertips to separate.

3) This movement indicates full use of the lungs, resulting in a truly deep breath rather than the "puffed chest" breath experienced by many as the greatest lung capacity. Chest breathing fills the middle and upper parts of the lungs. Belly breathing is the most efficient method. Infants and small children use only this method until the chest matures. The yoga breath or roll breathing combines belly and chest breathing.

For best results, practice this exercise for 5 minutes.

Energizing your body

Try this exercise before going out to do your horse. It can really help to energize your body and make you feel ready to ride.

1) Sit comfortably on a chair, somewhere you won't be disturbed.

2) Place your feet firmly on the floor. Let your attention rest on the connection between your feet and floor.

3)   Become aware of the energy in your feet and ankles rising up through your body. Feel how your feet are connected to your ankles.

4)   Let your attention rest on your lower legs, feel the energy rising up through your feet, through your ankles and to your lower legs.

5)   Become aware of your knees, feel how your knees are connected to your lower legs and thighs; feel the energy rising up through your feet, ankles, and lower leg to your knees.

6)   Let your attention rest on your thighs, feel the energy rising up further, from your feet, to your lower leg and up into your thighs.

7)   Become aware of your hips and waist, feel how your legs are connected to your body; feel the energy rising up through your legs and into your body.

8)   Let your attention rest on your heart and chest area; feel the energy flooding into your heart and chest, spreading all over your body.

9)   Become aware of your neck and head, feel how your neck is connected to your body and head, feel the energy rising through your body, up through your feet, into your legs, up into your body and into your neck and head.

10)   Let your attention rest on your shoulders, arms and hands, feel how each are connected to each other and feel the energy running down your arms.

11)   Now, starting from your feet feel the energy rise up through your body invigorating your muscles, up to your head and down through your arms.

12)   As you breathe in feel the energy rise through your body and as you breathe our feel the energy spreading around your body energizing every part.

This is another exercise that may take some practice, however, it is worth practising and putting the time in to feel energy or chi running throughout your body, giving you energy and making you feel good.

Teaching children

The children currently learning to ride are our next generation of horse riders and owners, how great would it be, if these children can understand the concept of working with energy with the horse from a young age, so it stays completely natural to them, instead of being conditioned out of them.

We can use Reiki or energy exercises but 'jazz' them up a little bit for children, to make them interesting and of something that they can relate to.

Follow The Yellow Brick Road

When children are riding ponies that nap or perhaps do not want to go the same way as the child or maybe they are just having a bit of fun, I like to use the golden energy trail.

Instead of just asking the child to follow a golden trail of energy like I have explained in the previous exercises, I ask them to follow an imaginary yellow brick road. So, say if the child is having trouble getting the pony to go into a corner, I would say to imagine that they are on a special yellow brick road, it's a narrow road, so make sure you and the horse don't fall off it, however, it is a very safe road, so the horse feels very safe when following the path, a child can easily listen to this, as we are telling them a story, as they take in the story they are already setting their intentions and creating the energy as to where the pony is going to go.

The Solar Plexus: Open or shut?

Something I often see children doing, particularly if they have been scared whilst riding, is perching forward, completely closing off the solar plexus. This important energy centre, incorporates our sense of self and when the sense of self is diminished or closed on a horse, the child is conveying completely the wrong energy. In fact, I could go so far as to say that the horse very much dislikes it when one is hiding the solar plexus. Please note, I am not talking about being in jumping position or a light seat, I am talking about a perched look, where the stomach is scrunched up.

The good news is that this is actually quite easy to rectify. I tell the child (or adult) that they have an eye on their stomach, just below their chest, when they are 'crunched up', the eye is closed, however, when they sit up and stretch this area the eye is open. The eye brings confidence to the rider when it is open.

Lunging

People have different ideas of what 'good lunging is and people use lunging for different purposes, some use it as schooling, others to 'get the beans out' of the horse before riding – the list goes on. For me, it is important that the horse works truly on the circle, listens to what I ask and enjoys his work.

There are often issues with horses not staying on a true circle, they might fall out on one part of the circle and then fall in on another part, again here we can use the golden trail exercise, imagine the circle that the horse will easily follow, lay the trail for him to follow.

For horses that lack rhythm on the lunge, I would suggest singing to them or playing music with the correct beat to help the horse come to the desired rhythm. As you ask for trot, set the beat in your head before the horse makes the transition.

When a horse is lacking enthusiasm imagine the golden trail, but imagine it moving with the horse, ushering him along.

If a horse is too fast, you could imagine the golden trail, lift from the ground and encompass the horse, bringing calmness.

Reiki in stables/ horseboxes and other spaces

If a horse gets particularly upset by a situation, by being put in his stable for example, or loaded into a horse box, then we can use Reiki to create a good energy, atmosphere and feeling. To Reiki areas like a stable or horse box:

1) Sit or stand comfortably.

2) Connect to Reiki

3) Feel the energy build in your Tanden

4) As you breathe out flood the energy like bright light from your body and fill the space around you. This energy, lays softly on the areas around you, making the area feel nice to be in. At this stage you could use the CKR symbol instead,

simply drawing it on the walls of the horse box. CKR works well as a space cleanser.

Example

We had a sweet but slightly nervous cob gelding in for training. He hadn't had very much done with him on the handling side and wasn't keen on going into the stable. On first arriving at our yard we tried to put him into a stable, with his owners help, to no avail.

We left him in the yard whilst we sorted out the paper work, approximately half an hour later all was quiet so I thought I would try to put him in the stable on my own. I caught him up and opened the stable door. I then stood just inside the stable to the side, so that he had plenty of space to enter the stable. I held the end of the rope with no pressure on his head, and proceeded to fill the stable with Reiki. He walked straight in after 2 minutes maximum!

Example

When we train our foals to load we give them as much time as they would like, to sniff around the horse trailer, have a good look inside and nibble the tasty food on the ramp! On one occasion, my sister Vicky was with one of the youngsters letting her see the horse trailer. I was standing with my mum watching the young horse being inquisitive. As I stood there I decided to send Reiki to the horse trailer, with the intent of making it really inviting so that in turn the youngster would want to go in. I sent Reiki for around five minutes, at which time my mum turned to me and said "for some reason I really feel like going into the horse trailer"- funnily enough she didn't even know what I had been doing! Needless to say, the youngster went calmly into the horse trailer shortly afterwards.

Undesirable habits

Some habits can relate directly to riding, say not standing still whilst being mounted and some are found around the stable yard, although these are not directly related to riding, they do have an effect on how you feel about the horse, what you think about the horse, in turn making them very important in our relationship with the horse. For persons that are keeping their horse at livery, it can be quite annoying, if whilst trying to have a nice ride, a horse is banging the stable door.

When looking at these issues it is important to remember to let go off our preconceived image of the horse, in effect, we need to forget that we know the horse has an issue and start over. Any time that we think of the horse having an issue, we are feeding the issue, we are telling the horse to do it more.

Below I have described how to deal with some common issues found on yards:

Banging the stable door / Pawing whilst tied up
Imagine all four hooves connected to the ground, like tree roots sprouting from the hooves, these 'tree routes' bring calm energy and a lovely feeling for the horse standing still.

Biting wood/ wind sucking/ weaving

Visualise the horse standing calmly, with his head staying still over the stable door; imagine this feeling really nice for the horse. For horses crib biting, we can send Reiki to the objects they bite making them uninviting to bite.

Running through fences

We can visualise energy barriers to make the fence more off putting to the horse, just imagine a huge wall of energy where the fence is. This exercise works very well with our cremello mare, who has poor eyesight in certain lights, she had a tendency to run through electric fencing, after commencing with this exercise she stopped and backed off the fence with plenty of time to spare!

Breaking the rope whilst tied

We can put our intent on the energy, to make the horse feel nice whilst tied up, we can also imagine an energy wall behind the horse, so that it does not want to back up into the 'wall'. Or we could use our intent to make the post to horse connection strong, we think of the connection being unable to be broken.

In-hand work

Working with the horse in-hand in a situation can help just as much as going in full blown when riding, in fact it can be easier and safer to work with some things on the ground before relating to the situation whilst on board.

Most of the exercises in the this book can be used in-hand, ridden or distantly, however, I'd like to share with you an experience where it is easier to work from the ground with Reiki

Example

Oceano was 10 years old. He had recently been gelded due to an injury. When coming back into ridden work his rider found that he had changed from a highly schooled horse to feeling very green and unresponsive. Oceano had also decided that he didn't like going to the far end of the riding arena. His rider could tell him to and he would, but he wasn't happy about it and his way of going had really deteriorated.

For Oceano's first in-hand session, I asked to be left alone with him in the sand school. I left him free to roam and took a few minutes to view his chakras. The Root Chakra was quite dull – relating to home life and feeling secure. The Sacral Chakra seemed to be buzzing and fuzzy, just like a television when it is out of tune – relating to sexual organs. The Solar Plexus Chakra was good. The Heart Chakra was nicely shining however, I felt he wanted to be hugged and told he was loved. The Throat

Chakra was a little small – relating to communication. The Third Eye and Crown Chakra were both functioning nicely.

I spent a few minutes using my intent to visualise bringing the chakras to their optimum functioning, seeing them shining brightly.

After this I had the feeling that I should take Oceano to the far side of the arena which he didn't like. Oceano graciously lowered his head into the headcollar. I walked backwards a few steps, facing Oceano on the end of the rope, when we approached the middle of the arena Oceano stopped and planted himself, just as he would do when ridden. I gently pulled and released the rope a few times to encourage him, but he wasn't budging!

I stood with a loose rope and sent love to Oceano, I visualized a barrier of energy pushing along from behind, like a wave making a small piece of driftwood come towards me – as I did this he walked forwards. I rewarded this by sending more love, calming beautiful energy.

I then visualized beautiful golden energy all over the arena and used my intent to put an inviting comfortable feeling to the far end of the arena.

Oceano walked towards me a few more paces and then tears began to roll down my face. Oceano showed me that this was the area he covered his mares in whilst in-hand mating. He showed me that there was a lot of confusion energy which made him feel very uncomfortable, as he knew this was no longer a part of his life. He was pleased that I had washed the confusion energy away.

Oceano went on to show me that he felt unhappy at the moment as he felt that he was no longer seen as the 'Magnificent, wonderful, beautiful, stunning stallion' instead people saw him and felt worry. I told him this would change and then we continued to walk around the arena, passing through the area he didn't like.

When Oceano was ridden later that day he didn't react to the far side of the arena, he was forward and listened to what his rider asked.

Experience

Last summer I was invited to give a Reiki session to a horse who had come in from the field one morning with a fractured skull and who it appeared was not only suffering from the trauma of the injury but from his body language was also reliving the aftermath of previous injuries and trauma sustained earlier in his life as an eventer. At this point he was reluctant to eat and appeared very stressed when approached, naturally his owner was extremely anxious about his recovery and his health. The facial injuries were settling and he had received some physiotherapy to help with the recovery, but it was during that first Reiki session that we saw him truly relax and in fact he lay down in front of both myself, and his owner (a new experience for us both).

I followed up that first session with several weeks of distant healing, during which time I was very happy to hear reports of Monty's renewed appetite and a general return of interest in his life and work. I was asked to help exercise Monty at the end of the summer and worked with Reiki to prepare him before and during the ride out to the forest. Tacking up I sensed at some point had been an unpleasant experience for Monty so I decided to Reiki the saddle before using it. The ride will stay with me for a very long time as the connection with Monty during our stroll to the forest was immense and at one point during a canter stretch the connection felt so strong and the action effortless for both of us that I felt we were almost suspended in time and space. My daughter who was riding her mare alongside us reports that it was a magical picture to behold and she saw us within a bubble of bright light on a cloudy day.

Ten months down the line I still visit Monty for occasion sessions of Reiki and massage and it is wonderful to see how far he has moved on. He remains a very special friend to me as the Reiki I channeled for him that day in June not only led me to pursue Equine Reiki further with Sarah, but has also wonderfully sent Monty's owner on her own Reiki journey and self-healing!

After such an affirmation I now practice Reiki daily. I send Reiki ahead to lessons I may be teaching and to horses I visit to massage. I have used Reiki successfully to surround both horse and rider in a calming energy in situations which they may have potentially found to be stressful, such as a first hack out or on

competition day and I have also used Sarah's technique of 'bright lighting' the jumping course which works a treat!
 Julie Brazier

Using sound within our riding

We all know how singing can help our horse keep to a rhythm and relax, now we can take this one step further using the kotodoma.

The kotodoma are very old. The word kotodoma means 'word spirit' or 'the soul of language'. They are based on the ancient idea of the sacred power of speech.

Kotodoma are found in Shintoism, as invocations, in Buddhism as invocations and mantras in some aspects of Buddhism and in Martial Arts as a way of focusing Ki.

Usui taught his students to connect with the different energies through using the kotodoma, they predate the use of symbols within Reiki.

The Reiki kotodoma have four names; Focus, Harmony, Connection and Empowerment.

- The Focus kotodoma represents Earth Ki and is represented by CKR in the Western System
- The Harmony kotodoma represents Heavenly Ki and is represented by SHK
- The Connection kotodoma represents a state of oneness and is represented by HSZSN
- The Empowerment kotodoma equates with the energy of Usui DKM

Pronunciation

The basic sounds:

A   aaah

O   as in rose

U   as in true

E   as in grey

I   eee

Kotodoma Name	Corresponding Reiki Symbol	The Sound	Pronounciation Guide
Focus	CKR	ho ku ei	Hoe koo eeee Ho rhymes with so, dough. Ku rhymes with too, moo
Harmony	SHK	ei ei ki	Ey eee ey eee keee Ki rhymes with see, tree
Connection	HSZSN	ho a ze ho ne	hoe aaah zay hoe neigh

			Ho rhymes with so, go
			Ze and Ne rhyme with day, say
Empowerment	Usui DKM	a i ko yo	aaah eeee coe yo
			Ko rhymes with so, go
			Yo rhymes with so, dough

Before working with the horse using the kotodoma it is a good idea for you to become accustomed to the use of them first:

1) Sit or lie down somewhere comfortable

2) Focus your attention on your Tanden

3) Take a few deep breaths and feel yourself becoming relaxed; your mind clearing

4) Chant the kotodoma on each out breath, using a deep, resonant voice

5) Vibrate the kotodoma from your Tanden, resonate the sound through your whole body; becoming the sound

6) Do this for a few minutes, and when you have finished chanting, just be still, enjoy the energy

7) Continue in this state for as long as feels appropriate.

Using the kotodoma in horse riding

The kotodoma can be used by chanting them silently to yourself or out loud. I have found that they seem most powerful out loud, however, there are certain situations where you may prefer to chant them in your head, so that passersby do not think you are crazy!

If you or a client would like to improve the connection between horse and rider the Connection Kotodoma can bring wonderful results

Experience

The first time I used the Connection Kotodoma on my horse was magical. I didn't actually feel that I needed to use it, but just wanted the practice and to see if there was a reaction. I thought I already had a good riding relationship with my stead, however, I hadn't realised just what could be achieved so simply. I got on and just asked my horse to stand, then I began chanting, my horse was very still so I carried on for a few minutes, still nothing, my horse seemed uninterested. Then I thought, we had better get on and have some exercise, in that instant my horse walked on, I had literally just thought of this, he picked it up at the moment I was thinking it and even better, he acted accordingly. This carried on throughout the session, I didn't have to do anything for the whole ride, I was just a passenger, but the horse responded to my every thought and intent.

When I had finished, I suddenly realised that a group of liveries had stopped to watch me, I would normally become a bit tense with others watching and judging me, but I hadn't even noticed! As I dismounted and walked over to the gate, we were congratulated on our performance, one lady said that we looked as if we were making our own song.

Needless to say, I use the Kotodoma whenever I have a chance to, I find it amazing, enjoyable and animals seem to really respond to it.
Caroline Ford

The Harmony Kotodoma is very useful for producing exactly that: harmony between horse and rider, but also harmony in body and mind.

Experience

I have been using the harmony kotodoma each time I get on my horse Orange. She can be a little cold backed, in that she raises her back up and becomes tense when being mounted.

I used the kotodoma every day for one week. I would start by silently chanting it to myself whilst walking into the arena; then as I stood by her head I would begin to say it loud, say three times. I then moved to the stirrup, repeating the chant over and over whilst I mounted and for around one minute whilst on board.

Over the course of a week Orange has really improved, she still tenses very slightly, but she doesn't raise her back up to the degree it usually would be and I feel much safer. Adding more to this I feel that this has developed a better understanding between Orange and I. Thank you Reiki!

James Thompson

The Focus Kotodoma can be used to bring inner strength to our handling and riding abilities, persons who think that their horse is not listening to their requests find this chant useful.

Experience

My youngster was being a little difficult; he was barging into me whilst being led. At the same time he hadn't had very much handling and was a bit nervous of people and very sensitive to the smallest of reactions.

I felt at a loss, I didn't want to put him off, but at the same time, I felt that I was teaching him bad habits, it wasn't his fault, I began to question myself, thinking am I doing the right thing, this only made matters worse and he began to circle round me and jump in the air in the following sessions.

Sarah suggested that I could try chanting the Focus kotodoma, to give me inner strength and to fill my aura with the energy, making it strong so that he wouldn't want to run in to me.

I put the headcollar on and then stood outside the stable chanting, building this energy in my aura; luckily no one was around as they may have thought I had lost the plot!

After a few minutes I felt it was time to 'try it out', I wasn't expecting a miracle, but it felt like one! He still had a bit of a prance, but he kept out of my space. I have carried on with the kotodoma with great results in all areas. If when riding, leading or grooming one of my horses, a kotodoma comes into my head I will just begin to chant and it really helps the situation
Shelly Banks

The Empowerment Kotodoma can be useful in restarting a situation. So say if you have had an issue and felt that you have exhausted all routes in how to deal with it, try the Empowerment kotodoma, it seems to have the ability to lift things away and allow you to start over with something. This can also be helpful if you have come to a block or standstill in training.

Experience
I had been in dressage training for many years, receiving advice from many coaches and riding in competitions, I felt that we

weren't progressing any more, in fact the more I thought about it, I felt that we hadn't progressed for some time.

I decided to try the Empowerment kotodoma, I stood in the stable with my horse and imagined us doing dressage, then I began to chant the Empowerment kotodoma, I couldn't say how long I chanted for as I seemed to be somewhere else. I felt that my horse and I had gone to a different place, but that is all I can remember. When I came round from the connection and back to normality, I went to my horse and stroked his lovely neck, WOW, suddenly realizations began coming to me in flashes, one of which I don't mind sharing here, was that neither of us had been enjoying dressage, I had become frustrated all the time and not enjoyed any of it and neither had my horse.

Although I suppose in one sense you could say that it didn't work as I didn't get past my block in the dressage field.... Instead I realised that I didn't want to do dressage any more, not in a competitive or serious way, instead I wanted to enjoy my time with my horse. We began to hack out more, on our second hack I met another rider, we rode together for a while and she told me all about the pleasure rides she took part in. It sounded just what we needed, however, I didn't own a horsebox. Sharon offered to take both horses, it turned out that her horse was a little unsettled to travel, so it was easier to travel them together.

Sharon's horse now travels like a dream next to my boy and we regularly take part in pleasure rides. Although a bit surprising I couldn't be more happy with the way things have turned out.
Alison Bates

Further use of symbols

The Fire Dragon

This symbol is drawn, starting at the top from the left and then drawing the weave, from top to bottom.

The balancing effect of this symbol seems to be geared to the needs of the individual, rather than producing a standard balance.

To use this symbol on yourself, draw or visualize the symbol with the horizontal over the crown chakra, with each curve encasing

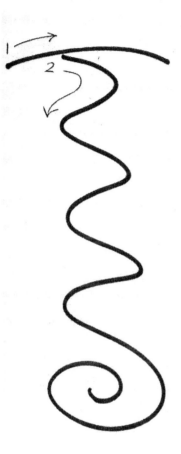

each of the seven chakras and empowering them. The symbol finishes over the root chakra, where it stops and spirals.

For use on a horse, visualisation is usually necessary, starting above the crown/ poll and weaving along the spine of the horse to the root chakra. When visualizing this symbol I like to draw it slowly, seeing each chakra glow as it comes into contact with the symbol.

If drawing the symbol physically, you can then push it into the body, or visualize it entering the body.

The name does not need to be chanted for this symbol, just draw and hey presto!

The Mental Spiral

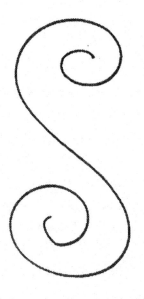

This symbol works on the mental aspect, but seems to penetrate deeper than SeiHeKi.

To use on yourself you would draw or visualize the fist part of the symbol over the forehead and trace the remainder over the crown towards the back of the head.

To use on a horse it is usually easier to visualize the symbol, starting over the forehead, and finishing over the poll.

To draw this symbol, start with the upper spiral and make your way down.

The top spiral represents the higher consciousness. The bottom spiral represents subconscious.

Manifestation techniques for horse riding.

Below I have included a meditation for manifesting goals, in this context we will discuss the meditation for use in horse riding; however, you can change the words to help you manifest your desires.

1) Find some where quiet and comfortable to relax
2) Close your eyes and breathe slowly, thinking of Reiki
3) Just allow the energy to come down to your Tanden and spread throughout your body
4) Now begin to imagine yourself in the situation that you desire.
5) Begin to add colour to the images, making them more real.
6) Now begin to feel how you would if the situation happened. Smile whilst thinking.
7) Let your subconscious believe that you are in that situation now, take time to enjoy it
8) Let your attention fall back to your Tanden, take some deep breaths and open your eyes.

If possible try to imagine that you are in this same situation throughout the day, just a couple of minutes here and there. You will get out, what you put in with this exercise.

Colour therapy

Just like Chakras, Colour Therapy isn't strictly Reiki, however, it is something really simple that you can use on yourself and your horse, so I would like to include a little information about it.

If you enjoy working with the chakras, you can use colour therapy to aid the balance of a chakra which is sluggish say. This is very simple in that you would just use that colour on the horse, so say if his root chakra was not at its optimum functioning, you could use a red numnah, headcollar, browband, boots, rug on the clothing side. You could also use foods that are red, so say a red apple each day, or some rosehip tea in his feed.

 We can also work with colours intuitively, so have a look at the colours that your horse has within his belongings, use this list to mark how many items of each colour he has out of

- red

- orange

- yellow,

- green

- blue

- indigo

- violet

-   magenta

Ignore the colour black as this enhances the other colours you are using, rather than eliciting a 'colour energy'.

The colour white contains all of the colours in the spectrum, so is a good add on.

When you look at the colours you use on your horse, and in this list I mean everything, from food bowls, hoof picks, grooming brushes, rugs and so on. You will most likely find that one or two colours are a bit lacking, these are the colours that will help your horse. You see you are intuitively picking up the colours that match with the colours your horse is portraying and kitting him out with those colours – even though you may not have been aware of it!

Experience

When Sarah first told me about colour therapy, I thought that sounds interesting, but doesn't really apply to my horse, he's ok and I couldn't think of any colours I didn't want to put on him. When I got home that night, I made the horses their feed, I moved the feed bowls round and realised I had moved them around so that I didn't give my horse the yellow one – I wanted to give my horse the red, I suddenly got goose bumps as I realised that I had always done this.

I felt my body begrudgingly give my horse the yellow feed bucket. I then went and dug out an old yellow numnah. After a week of doing this I noticed that he was freer than usual in his paces, he is quite old now, so I thought the stiffness was just something that would be apparent in an old horse, but now he is more like a 6 year old than a 26 year old!
Debbie Kirk

Colours can also help in other ways, for example, red can be associated with security, so if you feel nervous when riding, try wearing something red, this could be a top, scarf, gloves, socks anything you would like.

Below I have included a list of what colours can relate to, I hope you enjoy trying this out.

Red – stimulating, courage, sense of security, will-power, determination, independence, physical strength, competition, speed and assertiveness.

When a person or horse has an aversion to red, they may be aggressive too impulsive, egocentric, and over-active or they may have difficulties with people or other animals who display these characteristics.

Orange - optimism, success, stimulation, energy, achieving goals and encouragement.

When a person or horse has an aversion to orange they may be materialistic or indulgent. They may have suppressed sexual feelings or have issues with the sensual enjoyment of life.

Yellow – enhances mobility, progress, joy, cheerfulness, vitality, change, learning, mental clarity, concentration and communication,

When a person or horse has an aversion to yellow: it can mean they are emotionally disappointed, change activities often and may have a tendency to rationalise feelings.

Green - rejuvenation, balance, recovering, harmony and peace.

When a person or horse has an aversion to green they may prefer to be independent rather than having close family friends around.

Blue - Peace, understanding, calmness, patience and loyalty.

When a person or horse has an aversion to blue, they may not like restriction, lots of noise or persistant talking.

Indigo - can help mental problems, anxiety and panic. It can also help with issues relating to the eyes and ears.

When a person or horse has an aversion to indigo, it can mean their mind is very busy, they may find it hard to deal with stressful situations.

Violet - inspiration, counter-acts depression, rebalances the hormonal system and nervous disorders.

When a person or horse has an aversion to violet they may have a serious attitude towards life or they may dislike things which are unnatural or unrealistic.

White - (inner) peace, inspiration.

When a person or horse has an aversion to white they may only be interested in tangible objects. They may dislike subjects which are not fully understood.

Magenta - extra power, life purpose, life path.

When a person or horse has an aversion to magenta they may dislike being with people who have strong emotions.

Equine Articles

Pride in Being

A few years ago, someone named me as egotistical because I so much enjoyed and took pride in the way my horse showed himself off. At the time I was taken aback, as having a major ego issue hadn't been something I had identified myself with. The person told me all the 'right' things about how the ego 'worked' and I began to feel guilt that I should take so much enjoyment at he joyous 'here I am' being of my equine pal.

On arriving home, it was time for contemplation... Should I be feeling this? Am I a bad person? What do people think of me? The list goes on...

As I sat and pondered, I decided to meditate, I visualized myself with my horse, staying completely passive as he showed himself off. Something wasn't right, the horse began to look limp and loose his 'x-factor'.

And that is when it clicked; horses love to be admired, all animals love to be admired, I'm not talking about just saying words of "he's nice" or "she's going well", I mean the energy we emit when we see something beautiful, the energy that is transmitted as our breath is taken away, when a tear comes to our eye, when our body tingles with pure love at the sight and feel of true beauty.

I realised that is not egotistical to admire the union between myself and my horse, it is something that should be loved and enjoyed. It wasn't egotistical, because I wasn't comparing, thinking 'we're so much better than others'. I was enjoying the moment and conscious of the enjoyment my horse and I were having, it was just us, there and then, nothing else existed; only that beautiful connection.

This bought more questions to my attention… animals respond, develop and mature to the slightest feeling of love and admiration; so what it going on with people??!! We are constantly judging ourselves; weight, looks, graying hairs, wrinkles – when we should be following in the footsteps of our animal friends, admiring ourselves, loving ourselves, loving every imperfection which makes us who we are.

What do you see when you look in the mirror?

I have a task for you, go and look in the mirror, look deep into your eyes and smile, see yourself smiling back at you, look at each part of your body, look deep and smile, allow your whole body to smile.

Feel that energy coming from your body, transmitting to everything around you. Smile and the world smiles back!

Believe in yourself: have confidence.

Many riders have worries and doubts about their ability to be the best rider that they can; you may always think that others are better than you or that you will never get to 'that' stage you have always dreamed of.

Although building your confidence slowly over time can gradually allow you to be believe in yourself, the following meditation can really help to clear doubts:
- Close your eyes, allow your mind to become clear and connect to Reiki,
- Allow your doubts of riding ability to rise, ask to feel these doubts and greet them as they surface.
- Allow yourself to really feel these doubts - don't try to block them out, really feel them, feel if there is a particular place in your body where they are residing.
- By really feeling your doubts you are able to accept them, once you have accepted them, they don't affect you - they don't affect you because you have accepted that your thoughts are just a part of you, they don't control you.

It is what some call the 'negative ego' rising in you saying "you can't do this, you're not good or special enough", when this feeling rises smile at it, you have recognised it for what it is - which is just a thought, it's not a reflection of your abilities, it is just a thought and you as a person have the ability to control your thoughts.

Mindfulness and Compassion

In this article I want to talk to you about Mindfulness and Compassion, which I believe are two essential components of Reiki practice. Whether we are treating others, working on ourselves, empowering others or living our lives with Reiki, we should grow to embody these two states, the essence of the Reiki precepts.

According to Usui Sensei's surviving students, Mindfulness was taught at First-Degree level, and emphasized further at Second Degree. Mindfulness is a state of living in the moment, of being relaxed, calm and fully engaged in what we are doing. Mindfulness is being aware of what is happening right now and giving ourselves completely to our task without distraction. By learning how to enjoy and be in the present moment we can find peace within ourselves.

I believe we are exhorted to achieve this state by the precepts, where "just for today" we release anger and worry. These are distractions. We don't dwell on the past and beat ourselves up for the things that did not go the way we wanted, we do not think about the future and worry about things that have not yet happened. Our reality is illusion. We can learn to release our attachments to the past and the future and just "be" now, content and accepting in the moment. For me, the precepts represent a goal to work towards, and a description of the effects that Reiki can produce within us, over time, if we work with the energy in a committed, dedicated way.

The final precept, that of being "compassionate towards ourselves and others" is for me an exhortation to be gentle with ourselves, to be patient, to be light-hearted, to not take ourselves quite so seriously and above all to be forgiving – first of all of ourselves but also of others. By accepting and forgiving ourselves we start to release our anger and our worry, and move towards a state of contentment in the moment.

The original system was a spiritual path, a path to enlightenment, and the precepts were what Usui Sensei's system was all about. These principals are a foundation for everything we do with Reiki;

the states of mindfulness and compassion arise from following the precepts and from working with Reiki.

For example, how do we feel when we carry out a Reiki treatment? Treating someone with Reiki is a special, special gift. We feel a closeness, an intimacy, a merging with the recipient; we receive trust and we experience compassion. Ideally we should just be there in the moment, with the energy, with the recipient, with no expectations. We do not treat someone with the intention to resolve their health problem of eliminate their headache. We just merge with the energy and allow Reiki to do its work. We create a sacred space for healing to occur. If our mind wanders, as it may do, then we notice this and gently but firmly bring our attention back to the present and what we are doing. We become one with the energy as it flows through us, we become one with the recipient, and we experience that blissful contentment in the moment.

Though some are taught that you can hold a conversation with someone as you treat, or watch television at the same time, this really will not lead to the best being given to the recipient. To be the most effective channel we can be, we need to be there with our energy, fully and gently engaged in our work, giving ourselves fully to the task without distraction.

Those same principals apply when working on ourselves, whether carrying out Hatsurei ho or self-treating. The state we should seek to achieve is that of being fully engaged in the endeavour, of being with the energy without distraction, merged, aware and simply existing in the moment, with a gentle feeling of forgiveness, love and compassion towards ourselves.

So both Mindfulness and Compassion are fundamental to our life with Reiki, fundamental to the Reiki precepts, to working on others and working on ourselves. Not surprisingly they are also an essential component of the transmission of Reiki to another person through carrying out Reiju Empowerments. Reiju is the 'connection ritual' that Usui Sensei used, and taught to his surviving students. It is simple, elegant and powerful, free from the clutter and detail that surrounds most Western attunement styles. When we perform Reiju we have no expectations: we are there in the moment with the energy, following the prescribed movements. We are relaxed and fully engaged in what we are doing, aware of what is happening right now, and we give ourselves completely to our task without distraction. That is the essence of Reiju, the essence of treatments, the essence of the precepts, and the essence of our life with Reiki.

Article by Taggart King, www.reiki-evolution.co.uk

Questions and Answer Section

Below are some questions that have been asked of me, that may be of interest to you…

How do you ride without a saddle and bridle?
Firstly, let me just say, we do not just get on the horses without tack or any prior training – although some of them we most probably could have!

Instead we progress to this, being in harmony with the horse so that you can ride without tack has always been the ultimate riding in my mind.

We start by doing extra stretches, to make our own body more supple and able to sit lightly, with comfort and ease on the horses' back.

We then move this on to riding bareback. After we can walk, trot, canter, stop and steer without loss of balance bareback and without any use of rein, just through seat and intent, we will ride bareback in a head collar with reins attached to either side of the noseband.

Again we are looking that the horse listens to us in just a head collar – this may seem unnecessary, as we have already achieved this without any use of the bridle, however, the horse will know that he has a head collar on and we need to see if he is going to act differently. We may try some gymkhana games, going in and out of cones and stopping at the end.

After this stage we rely on our intuition to tell us when we are ready to ride free – and off we go!

NB It is very handy to use HSZSN or the Connection kotodoma during the above exercise.

Whilst working on the chakras I saw what appeared to be a black hole where the heart chakra would be, what does this mean and what should I do?

This simply means that the heart chakra needs Reiki, one can put labels on this such as it is blocked or closed, but you need not worry about the labels, just send Reiki to bring the chakra to it's optimum, when you see the chakra shining brightly, move on to the next chakra.

The people at the livery yard where I keep my horse seem to ruin my time with her. I like to have fun, go for hacks and take part in small RC shows; however, they make me feel that I should be trying for more, instead of having fun. Is there anything I can do

to stop them making me feel down? I have tried sending Reiki to myself to be able to deal with them better, but I just wish they would leave me alone!

This is actually quite common, so don't worry you are not alone. There are so many people that would like to tell you what to do, when really they need to focus on what they are doing themselves. On the Reiki side of things, I would send Reiki to help the situation, imagine yourself riding round and feeling happy, I should think that at the moment, each time you think of riding, you are probably also thinking of the people you are having to deal with, so start afresh. Now is the time to imagine riding and having fun, people just getting on with their own stuff and not bothering you. Do this visualisation each day for a week and see how things are going.

I've heard that you should not give Reiki before riding, is this correct?

I tend not to give a full treatment before riding as the horse generally would like a nice rest afterwards. Some horses may like some gentle exercise later on in the day, particularly if they are stabled, just having some time to walk around and stretch their legs.

For the most effective treatments, I have found not exercising after a Reiki treatment to be most beneficial. Usually by the next day the horse is ready to be ridden again.

Although I wouldn't give a full treatment, what one can do is to use their intent, so say send Reiki with intent that the horse is going to be calm whilst ridden, or using SHK whilst he is being ridden to help with his anxieties.

I've been taught to always ask permission from the animal before giving Reiki to him/her, why don't you include this in your instructions?

If you feel that you want to or you 'should' ask permission then go ahead and do it, it's not hurting anyone, follow what feels right for you. The reason I don't feel the need to ask for permission, is that I would then be putting the horse on a lower level, not giving him credit for his intelligence or energy sharing abilities. You can't force an animal to share Reiki with you, they choose, so in effect when you begin to send out Reiki, you are offering the connection to the horse, I like to offer the energy whilst it's there, the horse senses this and decides whether to connect. At the same time if you feel that you are doing wrong by not asking for permission first, the horse will probably not connect, as the energy you will be offering will be filled with anxiety or wrong doing. So my answer to this question is to do what feels right for you.

I see in some of your photos you carry whips, people should not have whips around horses, they are cruel, do you not think this sends the wrong impression?

I do not feel that whips are cruel, to me a whip is an extension of my arm, so say if I am leading a stallion and the stallion raises his head I will raise my whip, this isn't towards him or flapping about but simply in my hand parallel to him, mirroring what he has done. This makes my height increase to the same height as the stallion. During riding, I carry a whip sometimes as a refined aid, so say if I would like the horse to give a little more impulsion, I can just touch him with the whip, the lightest touch, the whip I carry is long so that it reaches his back end, the horse would much prefer to be touched lightly on the backend than to be kicked in the girth area, or shoved by the seat.

I wonder what the difference is between a whip and a twig from a tree? It is the intent put on the object, not the object itself, the person makes the object good or bad, in my opinion.

- I can see where you are coming from but, the Greater Consciousness of whips is too great to overcome, the Greater Consciousness sees whips as bad, they will always be seen as bad from a horses' point of view.

If this was the case all or the vast majority of horses would be scared of whips, which isn't the case. My belief is that we are here to raise the vibration, so if you feel that whips are bad, you need to ask yourself why and heal that place in your body which is holding

156

the fear, raise your own vibration to overcome limiting beliefs - we can overcome anything, just believe.

There are people on the yard who smack their horses, how would you approach the situation to tell them what they are doing is wrong? Horses don't understand violence and it breaks my heart to see this.

This is a phrase I have heard a lot recently "horses don't understand violence". I'm not sure where it has come from, but I have quite some trouble in believing it. The first thing a mare does to her foal when he doesn't go where he is told it to bite him, to say "listen". Horses will kick, bite, swish, charge at another when he needs to be put back in his place in the herd. So for me horses do understand violence, however, this violence is forgotten straight away. The horse doesn't stay angry. It is over and done with, mission complete.

At the same time I do not think that violence from human: horse or horse: human is a good thing! I would much prefer to see nice training, allowing the horse to learn how we would like him to behave and for the horse to choose to do so because he wants to follow us, this is done simply by being a fair leader and loving companion.

Something that the horse doesn't understand is when we try to hide emotions. Horses understand emotions and obviously feel them freely, acting accordingly, but they dislike when a person is suppressing emotions. The person may feel that they are being strong, because they are trying to deal with what is going on, without showing what they are feeling, trying to act normally, even when they are hurting inside. The horse thinks the person is crazy – and would rather be a few miles away! Yet if we are honest and open with the horse about our feelings he will want to come to you, be close and support you.

There are a couple of answers to your questions. Number one, is to tell the owner straight, which sometimes needs doing, particularly in cruelty cases, however, the owner in question, is probably dealing with their own problems, has a lot of frustration and the horse is bringing this out – horses are great at multiplying emotions!

Perhaps try and help the owner, offer some Reiki, send Reiki to the horse and owner relationship and also send Reiki to the situation. Let the owner know that you are willing to listen and to also help her with her horse; people are present in our lives for a reason. Maybe this person has arrived in your life in order for you to help them in some way.

Further Reading

Below I have included some of my favourite books on Connecting with Horses and Reiki. I am sure you will enjoy them!

Books

Dancing with Horses – Klaus Ferdinand Hempfling

The Horse Seeks Me, *My Way of Body Language* – Klaus Ferdinand Hempfling

What Horses Reveal, *From first meeting to friend for life* – Klaus Ferdinand Hempfling

Reiki 1st Degree Manual: Shoden – Taggart King

Reiki 2nd Degree Manual: Okuden – Taggart King

Reiki Master Teacher manual: Shinpiden - Taggart King

The Handbook of Equine Reiki – Sarah Berrisford

The Complete Guide to Animal Reiki – Sarah Berrisford

You Can Heal Your Life – Louise L. Hay

The Secret – Rhonda Byrne

DVDs

Dancing with Horses – Klaus Ferdinand Hempfling

The Celestine Phrophecy – James Redfield

Carry me wild horse without saddle or rein,
Free we will ride through the forest and plains,
I guide you by thought, as we travel with speed,
The feeling is deep, great the need,

You see within me in the moment we meet,
The truth I could not hide from thee,
Accepting what I am to join your game;
In the dance of life we are free

Lightning Source UK Ltd.
Milton Keynes UK
UKOW05f0301260717
306007UK00002B/93/P

9 780956 316875